Hayling Lifeboats

G000272472

Nicholas Leach

The following companies and organisations have kindly sponsored the production of this book and are proud to support Hayling Island lifeboat station:

Stannah Lifts Holdings Ltd

The Haven Trust

The Inn Shore Cruising Club

Brian Morrisey & Sons LLP

Dean & Dyball Civil Engineering Ltd

Wyche Marine, Dell Quay

Marina Developments Ltd

Northney Marina Berthholders Association

Studio Four Architects Ltd

Emsworth Yacht Harbour Ltd

HAYLING ISLAND LIFEBOAT STATION

First established 1865

Current lifeboat house opened in 2007
and designed by
STUDIO FOUR ARCHITECTS LTD

Engineered by
MAYHEW CALLUM LTD CONSULTING ENGINEERS

Built by
DEAN & DYBALL CIVIL ENGINEERING LTD

Contents

ISBN 9780951365694
© Nicholas Leach 2010
The rights of Nicholas Leach to be identified as the Author
of this work have been asserted in accordance with the
Copyrights, Designs and Patents Act 1988. All rights reserved.
No part of this book may be reprinted or reproduced or utilised
in any form or by any electronic, mechanical or other means,
now known or hereafter invented, including photocopying and
recording, or in any information storage or retrieval system,
without permission in writing from the publishers.

Published by Foxglove Media
Foxglove House, Shute Hill, Lichfield, Staffs WS13 8DB
t > 01543 673594
e > foxglove.media@btinternet.com

Layout and design by Nicholas Leach
Printed by Cromwell Press Group, Wiltshire, UK

Acknowledgements • This book could not have been written
without the help and support of Cdr Conrad Davies, who
patiently answered many questions, found a huge amount
of information and photos for inclusion and was the driving
force behind the project's success. I gladly acknowledge
the work of Jeff Morris, Honorary Archivist to the Lifeboat
Enthusiasts' Society, whose previous history of the station was
of considerable use during the preparation of this book. The
pioneering research into lifeboat history by the late Grahame
Farr has also been of use. Thanks also to Lifeboat Operations
Manager Nigel Roper, who has been extremely helpful and
hospitable during my visits to the station, and whose time
is most appreciated; to Graham Raines who assisted with
information; to Andrew Filipinski for supplying photographs;
and to the current lifeboat crews of Hayling Island. At RNLI
Headquarters in Poole, thanks to Brian Wead and his staff at
the Service Information Section, Nathan Williams and Eleanor
Driscoll for supplying images, and Liz Cook, Editorial Manager.

Introduction

The Royal National Lifeboat Institution (RNLI) opened the lifeboat station on Hayling Island in 1865 and pulling lifeboats were operated for almost sixty years. After flank stations at Bembridge and Selsey received motor lifeboats, Hayling Island was closed in 1924. During the 1960s, when recreational sailing expanded, a new rescue service started on the Island and this was later taken over by the RNLI. This book celebrates the combined 100 years of life-saving service by Hayling Island's lifeboats.

Since the RNLI stationed the first lifeboat on the Island nearly 150 years ago much has changed. The first two stations were on the sea front, but with the introduction of the inshore lifeboats a new location inside the harbour entrance best meets operational demands. Two inshore lifeboats are now operated and to house the launch and recovery tractors and our new Atlantic 85 the station has been adapted and extended. The new station handles an average of two 'shouts' a week, a considerable commitment for our volunteer crews. While we are proud of our history, and we still have one crew member related to a member of the first crew, we look forward to a bright future with a large, modern lifeboat house.

The generosity of the Hayling Island and Manhood fund-raising branches as well as all our harbour harbour community aremuch appreciated for, without their support, there would be no lifeboat station. And without the unqualified backing of our Island community, which provides funds as well as young men and women willing to voluntarily crew our lifeboats, there would be no lifeboat station. We are proud of our station, and are conscious of the high esteem in which it is held by the community.

The rescues performed by the pulling lifeboats at Hayling Island were predominantly in heavy weather to commercial shipping. They were often challenging for the crew, who showed strength and stamina using comparatively unsophisticated equipment. Since the station reopened, the situation has been totally different with numerous services, often more than

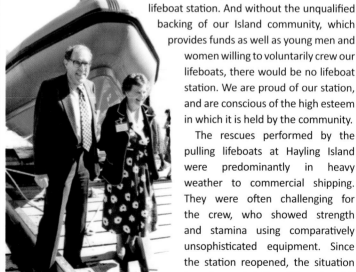

▲ Derrick and Betty Battle, Hayling Island lifeboat's main benefactors.

100 per annum, being undertaken, but the casualties are mostly recreational users of the sea in difficulty in inclement conditions. However, a number of very difficult rescues demonstrate that the inshore lifeboats and their crews are extraordinarily effective in arduous conditions. The list of awards speaks volumes for the dedication, courage and competence of today's crews.

Thank you for buying your copy of this book. The costs of production have been covered totally by our sponsors and the whole of your purchase money will go to RNLI funds to help continue the work of life-saving at sea.

Nigel Roper
Lifeboat Operations Manager

▲ The lifeboat house at Sandy Point, Hayling Island, as rebuilt in 2007, with Atlantic 85 and D class inflatable inshore lifeboats, and their launching tractors, outside being readied for a training exercise. (Nicholas Leach)

The challenges of the sea: a mariner's perspective

The seas, harbours and channels round Hayling Island presented many dangers and difficulties to nineteenth century vessels trying to navigate the area, and even for modern vessels with the latest electronic navigation aids the channels and banks can be challenging. Sailing craft approaching the entrances to Langstone or Chichester Harbours, in the prevailing wind, approached a lee shore, and the ability to beat offshore was limited. Lacking mechanical power and with only a small crew, nineteenth century sailing craft could easily get into difficulty, as anchor tackle was usually light with only limited holding ability in heavy weather. The low-lying shoreline had few distinguishing features, the positions of banks and shoals off each entrance were imperfectly known because they shift constantly, and few if any leading marks had been erected to guide vessels up the narrow entrance channels. Yet in the nineteenth century small ports such as Langstone, Emsworth, Bosham or Dell Quay, which are inside the harbour and insignificant by today's standards, were busy with little ships loading and unloading goods and commodities to trade to Europe or beyond.

The first lifeboat

The lifeboat station at Hayling Island was established during the latter half of the nineteenth century following a series of incidents which indicated a lifeboat was needed. The Island has Langstone Harbour and Portsmouth on its western side, Chichester Harbour on its eastern side and the English Channel to the south, and vessels could get into difficulty entering these harbours. However, the outlying sandbanks presented the main hazard to nineteenth century sailing craft, which were largely at the mercy of the wind and weather, and many were wrecked as a result.

One vessel that got into difficulty off the Hampshire coast was the sloop Cygnet, of Portsmouth, which was wrecked on 17 October 1862 in heavy seas and gale force winds. She had become unmanageable and ran aground on the Woolsiner Sandbank, which runs a mile and a half out from the mouth of Langstone Harbour. As the casualty started sinking, her three crew took to the rigging. Coastguards launched one of their boats and tried to reach the stranded men, but were defeated by the heavy seas. So three local fishermen, William Goldring, James Spraggs and David Farmer, went out in their fishing smack Ferret, which was taken as close as possible.

However, they could not reach the casualty in the heavy seas so they dropped anchor and launched the small rowing boat carried by the fishing boat. It was a feat of considerable strength and seamanship to then row through the heavy seas to the shipwrecked men, who were helped from the mast of their sunken vessel and into the small rowing boat, with one of them almost unconscious. The fishermen rowed to their smack, got the rescued men aboard it, and then landed them safely ashore. For their outstanding courage and bravery during this rescue, the three fishermen were awarded Silver medals by the Royal National Lifeboat Institution (RNLI).

Another shipwreck off Hayling Island that also resulted in the RNLI formally recognising the rescuers took place on 14 January 1865. Stormy weather over the previous few days had created heavy confused seas off the Island. During the morning the schooner Ocean, of Plymouth, while bound for Sunderland from Charleston, was pushed onto the Woolsiner Sandbank as her crew attempted to tack against the wind. Although they immediately let go both anchors, the vessel began bumping heavily on the shoal and quickly filled with water, forcing the five crew to take to the rigging.

The heavy seas that swamped the stranded vessel carried away two of her crew who were drowned. The steam tug Comet from Portsmouth was sent to help, but it could not get close enough in the shallow water to rescue the three remaining men. In such violent seas, the locals could only watch and pray that the three men could hold on until conditions improved.

When the tide turned, a large ten-oared cutter was launched from Fort Cumberland, Headquarters of the Royal Marine Artillery, manned by twelve fishermen chosen for their local knowledge. With Major F. W. Festing at the helm, they set off towards the wreck. At times, those on shore could not see the boat because of the severe weather. But with skill, great courage and outstanding seamanship, the cutter reached the wreck and the three men were saved. The journey back to the shore was equally hazardous, as huge waves battered the small boat, but they reached the shore safely and the three survivors were landed. For the outstanding gallantry displayed during this rescue, Major Festing was awarded the Silver medal by the RNLI.

At this time, the RNLI, the body founded in 1824 to organise a lifeboat service, was expanding its operations. The organisation had been founded under the title National Institution for the Preservation of Life from Shipwreck, and during the first three decades of its existence established lifeboat stations in the British Isles and Ireland. Its success was somewhat mixed, however, and by the 1840s its fortunes were at a low ebb, with the task of raising sufficient funds proving difficult.

However, during the 1850s a series of reforms was implemented, the service was renamed the Royal National Lifeboat Institution in 1854 and under new leadership greater revenues were generated to fund and expand the lifeboat fleet. Many new stations were founded around this time, most of which operated the RNLI's standard lifeboat design of the time, the self-righter. Hayling was part of this expansion, and during the first part of its operational life three self-righting lifeboats served the station.

▼ An engraving depicting the scene during the inauguration of Olive Leaf, Hayling's first lifeboat, 13 September 1865.

1865 – 1888

► An unusual old photo depicting the scene during the inauguration of Olive Leaf on 13 September 1865. (By courtesy of Hayling Island RNLI)

The Hayling Island station was established as a result of the events in 1862 and 1865 described above. The Rev Charles Hardy, Vicar of Hayling, wrote to the Hampshire Telegraph describing this and other shipwrecks in the locality, and also sent a letter to the RNLI in London urging that a lifeboat station be established on the Island. This letter was discussed by the Institution's Committee of Management on 2 February 1865 which agreed to establish a station. A week later the District Inspector visited the area to decide on the best site for a boathouse, and an order was placed with Forrestt's yard, at Limehouse in London, for a new self-righting lifeboat.

The tender submitted by H. R. Trigg for building a boathouse was accepted, and a house was constructed at the western end of the south shore of the Island for £259 10s 0d. A donation of £500 from Messrs Leaf & Sons, of London, was received towards the cost of setting up the station, and this was used to pay for the lifeboat, launching carriage and boathouse. The new lifeboat was a 32ft self-righter built of mahogany, with a launching carriage supplied by J. Robinson, of Kentish Town, at a cost of £86 8s 8d. The boat was ready by September 1865 and, after undergoing self-righting trials in Regent's Canal Dock, London, she was transported from London to Havant by the London and South Western Railway Co, free of charge.

The station was inaugurated on 13 September 1865, and the new lifeboat named the same day. A holiday was observed on the Island, with visitors coming from miles around to attend the special event. The ceremony started at 11am and, after a service of dedication, the Bishop of Chichester consecrated the boat, which was named Olive Leaf after the donor. At the end of proceedings, she was launched, cheered on by the crowd.

The first crew was formed by William Goldring, Coxswain, Thomas Spraggs, Second Coxswain and crew members Stephen Clark, Henry Barter,

Olive Leaf	
On station	September 1865 – April 1888
Record	10 launches, 32 lives saved
Donor	Messrs Leaf & Sons, London
Dimensions	32ft x 7ft 5in x 3ft 9in
Type	Self-righter, ten-oared
Cost	£258 1s 9d
Builder	1865, Forrestt, Limehouse
Disposal	Sold locally in 1889 for £10

Stephen Rogers, Snr, Stephen Rogers, Jnr, Stephen Goldring, Stephen Palmer, David Rogers, George Green, Edward Clark and Ebenezer Cole. The celebrations, which were held in the grounds of the country house of local land owner Mr Sandeman, continued throughout the afternoon and into the evening. Many of the local gentry, who had pledged their support for the new operation, were present, as was Major Festing. The Rev Hardy was appointed as Honorary Secretary of the new station.

During her twenty-three years on station, Olive Leaf is credited with saving more than thirty lives, although she only performed four effective services. On 29 October 1865 during a fierce storm, nine ships got into difficulties between Portsmouth and Hayling Island. Six of them cleared the shoals and headed into deeper water, but the schooner Favorite was driven onto the beach and became a total wreck. The 540-ton barque Atlas, of North Shields, was stranded on the Woolsiner Sands and Olive Leaf was launched through very heavy surf to assist. The lifeboatmen rescued her crew of thirteen, as well as one man from the Norwegian barque Sirius who had managed to get aboard Atlas after he and his colleagues had been forced to abandon ship.

On 1 February 1869 the Hayling Island lifeboatmen performed a very fine service after the barque Lady Westmorland, of Newcastle, ran aground on a sandbank close to the Church Rock during the early hours of the morning. In heavy seas and gale force winds, the vessel bumped heavily and started taking in water. Just as her crew were about to abandon ship, expecting their vessel to begin breaking up, Olive Leaf arrived. Some of the lifeboatmen boarded the barque and succeeded in getting the vessel off the sandbank and into harbour. They managed to save the vessel and her crew of eighteen.

Olive Leaf served at Hayling Island until 1888, launching four more times on service, but on each occasion no effective service resulted. Typical of these services was that on 20 November 1881 to the 405-ton barque Caducens, of North Shields. She launched, but as the wind was against her, did not reach the casualty until after its crew had been saved by another lifeboat.

▼ Olive Leaf being pulled across the sand dunes on her carriage for launching. She is remembered today by a pub on the seafront at Hayling Island called The Olive Leaf. (By courtesy of Hayling Island RNLI)

Charlie and Adrian

▶ The Rubie self-righter Charlie and Adrian returning to the beach. (From an old postcard supplied by Nicholas Leach)

In 1888 a new lifeboat was built for Hayling Island by Hansen & Sons at Cowes to replace the station's first boat, the self-righting ability of which was doubted. Provided out of an anonymous gift, which was later revealed to have come from Laurence Trent Cave, of Ditcham Park, a member of the RNLI's Committee of Management, the boat was named Charlie and Adrian after the donor's two sons. She was a 34ft ten-oared self-righter, and, as she was a little larger than her predecessor, she could not fit into the boathouse on her carriage. She therefore had to be launched over wooden skids across the beach, or manhandled onto her carriage outside the boathouse.

The new lifeboat arrived in April 1888 and was launched for the first time on service on 20 July, when she went to the barque Margit, of Norway, but her services were not required. She was called on again on 18 February 1889 when she helped a naval torpedo boat, but again no service resulted. Her first effective service took place on 14 January 1896 after the brigantine Marie Louise had gone aground on the Hounds Rock, west of Selsey Bill, while on passage from Falmouth to Hamburg. Charlie and Adrian was launched at 5.50am and stood by the stranded vessel until it refloated.

In September 1888 Charlie and Adrian had been sent back to her builder's yard to have a drop-keel fitted. Together with the water ballast tanks, this was one of a number of improvements in lifeboat

Charlie and Adrian

Official Number	146
On station	April 1888 – May 1914
Record	20 launches, 9 lives saved
Donor	Gift of L. T. Cave, Ditcham Park
Dimensions	34ft x 7ft 6in
Type	Self-righter, ten-oared
Cost	£347 9s 11d
Builder	1888, Hansen, Cowes
Disposal	Used as a display lifeboat

design of the time, and these items were the latest additions to make the boats better sailing craft. However, the drop-keel was not a total success as it could not be operated smoothly, so the lifeboat was sent to London in December 1889 for the keel to be altered at Woolfe's boatyard. After the modifications, the boat returned to station in May 1890.

Between 1897 and 1905 Charlie and Adrian was launched on service a number of times, but on each occasion her services were not needed. The vessels in difficulty included the schooner General Haverlock, of Portsmouth, on 2 April 1897; the ketches Georgina, of Poole, on 12 November 1900, and Seraphus, of Plymouth, on 2 March 1903; the cutter Dodo on 11 September 1903; and the motor yacht Cruban, of Glasgow, on 20 August 1905.

The lifeboat's next effective service took place on the morning of 8 February 1906. She was launched to the barge Mabel, of Portsmouth, which was on passage from Chichester Harbour to Portsmouth when she was caught in a heavy squall off Hayling Island. In the severe weather the vessel had been dismasted, so the master was forced to drop anchor and signal for help. Charlie and Adrian was launched at 11am, reached the barge forty-five minutes later, and then stood by. The south-westerly gale was accompanied by very heavy squalls, and a heavy sea was running, but the barge's master hoped he could save his vessel. A tug had been signalled for, but at 3pm no further help had arrived, so the master decided to abandon ship, as both he and the mate were suffering from exposure in the extreme cold. Both were taken into the lifeboat, which returned ashore and was rehoused by 5pm.

▼ Charlie and Adrian, with her crew on board, during her formal inauguration ceremony in 1888. Charlie Cave, the small boy with the collection box standing by the coxswain in the sternsheets, later became a member of the Committee of Management. (RNLI)

The next call came on 10 December 1909 after flares had been seen in the early hours from a vessel close to the Owers Lightvessel, six miles south of Selsey Bill and twelve miles from Hayling lifeboat station. Both lifeboats from Selsey and Hayling Island launched at about 3.30am to the ketch Birthday, of London, which was bound for Plymouth with a cargo of timber. Selsey lifeboat reached the casualty first, and once on scene the lifeboatmen found that her sails were torn, and the rudder-head, bowsprit and masthead of the mizzen were all broken. At the master's request, the lifeboat returned to shore to arrange for tug assistance, and then she put out again to stand by the ketch until the tug arrived from Littlehampton. On this occasion Charlie and Adrian was not required and so she returned to station.

A year later another launch which proved to be fruitless for the Hayling lifeboatmen was undertaken. On the afternoon of 13 December 1910, after the Italian brigantine Fratelli Lama got into difficulty during a strong south-westerly gale off Selsey Bill, lifeboats from Bembridge, Southsea, Selsey and Hayling Island all launched. Selsey lifeboat Lucy Newbons put out at 3.30pm in very heavy seas, which caused the brigantine to roll and pitch. Her crew stood by waiting for the tide to turn and conditions to ease. After standing by for several hours, the lifeboat was taken close enough to save the eight crew on the brigantine. Charlie and Adrian launched to the brigantine at 12.30am on 14 December, and made an effort to reach the casualty, but her services were not required and she returned to station.

However, this was not the last vessel to be caught out during the gale, which continued for several more days, with several lifeboats along the east and south coasts being called out. The call for Hayling Island lifeboat came on 16 December when, at 9.30am, the topsail schooner Blanche, of Dunkirk, bound to Lisbon with a cargo of corn, was seen in difficulties close to the

▼ Charlie and Adrian launching from her carriage with the crew ready at the oars. (By courtesy of Hayling Island RNLI)

◀ Three photographs of Charlie and Adrian being hauled back up the beach and into the 1865-built boathouse. They are in sequence, and were taken after a demonstration launch witnessed by onlookers dressed formally. These images give an idea of the difficulties of hauling the lifeboat up the beach by hand. Equally testing was actually powering the boat when she was at sea, and rowing against wind, sea and tide was a severe test for the crew. (By courtesy of Hayling Island RNLI)

Woolsiner Sands. Despite the severity of conditions, Charlie and Adrian was successfully launched at 10am through heavy surf pounding the beach at Hayling. In conditions later described by Coxswain George Miller and his crew as 'probably the worst we have been out in', the lifeboat succeeded in reaching the casualty, which had dropped two anchors but which were not holding in the heavy seas, and the vessel was drifting further into danger.

▶ The Rubie self-righter
Charlie and Adrian
returning to the beach.
(By courtesy of Hayling
Island RNLI)

The tug Empress, of Portsmouth, was standing by and, with the help of the lifeboatmen, a tow line was connected from the tug to the schooner. The anchors were slipped and, slowly, they set off for Portsmouth. Three times the cable parted so, with the schooner getting dangerously close to the shoals near Horse Sand Fort, it was decided to get the crew of seven off the schooner. Coxswain Miller took the lifeboat alongside the casualty with great skill, and the seven men were rescued. Although the lifeboat was damaged quite badly, she managed to return to Hayling Island where the rescued men were landed at 3pm. They were taken to the West Town Hotel, where they were treated for exposure, and it was found, according to the Hampshire Telegraph, that 'only one of them could speak even a little broken English'.

On 19 March 1913, during a bad storm along the south coast, several lifeboats launched to vessels in distress, including the Selsey boat, which stood by the ketch Gladys, aground on the Mixon Reef. Charlie and Adrian was called out at 8.30am to help the 200-ton three-masted schooner Rescue, of London, which was in difficulties two miles east of Chichester Harbour entrance having been caught in heavy seas and a south-westerly gale and gone ashore on Wittering sands. The lifeboat anchored about 400 yards off the schooner, but the crew could not see any signs of life aboard, so Coxswain Miller headed back to the shore.

However, conditions were so bad on the beach at Hayling Island, with the surf pounding the shore, that it was impossible to beach the lifeboat. She was taken across the bar, with considerable difficulty, and up to Chichester, where she was moored at 5pm. The crew, who returned to Hayling Island by road, were exhausted, but 'Mrs Crutwell showed them great kindness in providing dry clothing and food,' according to the Hampshire Post. When conditions improved the next day, they returned to Chichester and sailed the boat back to Hayling Island, beaching her there at noon. For this prolonged and arduous service, the RNLI made additional monetary awards to the crew, who consisted of Coxswain George Miller and Second Coxswain C. Cole

◀ Charlie and Adrian outside the 1865-built boathouse. This posed photograph shows her crew on board in their cork life-jackets, and the various station officials standing near the boat. (By courtesy of Hayling Island RNLI)

for the way they handled the boat. The other members of the crew on this service were E. Cole, G. Rowe, G. Jones, C. Boniface, E. Churcher, A. Austin, C. Bowers, W. Goldring, G. Goldring, H. Smart, and C. Cannings.

Charlie and Adrian launched for what proved to be the last time on service on 28 January 1914. She put out at 8.50am, within fifteen minutes of the firing of the maroon, after naval guns had been heard firing near the Nab Tower, the signal to indicate a vessel in distress. Dense fog obscured attempts to see what was amiss and, despite pulling for three and a half hours to undertake a thorough search of the area, the lifeboat could not find any vessel in need of assistance. When the fog lifted, the crew returned to station.

Charlie and Adrian was replaced at Hayling Island in 1914, but unusually she was not sold out of service. Instead, she was taken by rail on 17 June 1914 to Birmingham, where she was used for demonstration purposes and as a display lifeboat in one of the city's parks.

▼ The Hayling Island lifeboat crew, in front of Charlie and Adrian on her carriage. The kapok life-jackets they are wearing were introduced in 1904, and remained in use with RNLI crews for almost seventy years. (By courtesy of Hayling Island RNLI)

Proctor

▶ The scene at Hayling Island during the naming ceremony of Proctor in June 1914. Coxswain G. Miller (in cap) and Second Coxswain C. Cole can be seen sitting on the stern air box. Proctor was described on her arrival by the local newspaper as being 'the very latest thing in lifeboat construction, fitted with patent water ballast arrangements'. The crew were summoned by maroons, and a boy on a bicycle with a handbell was also employed for the same purpose. (RNLI)

The new lifeboat sent to Hayling Island arrived in May 1914. She was a 35ft Rubie self-righter, pulling ten oars and equipped with a jib, large mainsail and small mizzen. Rubie self-righters of this size were intended to be good sailing lifeboats, and fifteen of the class were built between 1906 and 1917. The boat for Hayling had been built partly by Thames Ironworks, and then completed by S. E. Saunders after Thames Ironworks went out of business. She cost £1,251 and was provided out of a gift from the late William John Proctor, of Newcastle, and was named Proctor. To accommodate her, an impressive new boathouse was built on the sea front adjoining the Coastguard station, about two miles east of the old house, at a cost of £900.

The new lifeboat was named on 9 June 1914 at the new boathouse in fine weather, with hundreds of spectators in attendance. The boat was taken on its carriage to the beach with the crew on board, led by Coxswain George Miller. After Vice-Admiral Sir James Startin, the Chairman of the station, gave a short speech about the work of the station since 1865, G. H. Proctor was introduced as the donor's representative. Lieut Basil Hall, Inspector for the south coast, accepted the boat on behalf of the RNLI, and handed it to the local committee. She was accepted by A. L. Stent, the station's vice chairman. After the service of dedication, the

Proctor	
Official Number	640
On station	May 1914 – 29 September 1924
Record	4 launches, 25 lives saved
Donor	Gift of John Proctor, Newcastle
Dimensions	35ft x 8ft 10in
Type	Rubie self-righter, ten-oared
Cost	£1,251
Builder	1914, Thames Ironworks, Blackwall; completed by S. E. Saunders, Cowes
Disposal	Sold 1934

lifeboat was officially named Proctor by Miss Proctor, and then launched for a short demonstration at sea under sail.

During the First World War, the Hayling Island lifeboat completed no effective services, but a number of personnel changes took place during this time. Captain R. W. Neate took over as Honorary Secretary at the start of 1916, and was succeeded in 1919 by Henry West. The same year George Miller retired as Coxswain due to ill health. He was replaced by Charlie Cole, a local fisherman who had been in the crew for a number of years, and Second Coxswain since 1901. His brother, Ernie, became Second Coxswain having served as Bowman for over eighteen years. Charlie Cole was a favourite with children who visited the station, giving them a penny if they were at the boathouse when the boat was launched on exercise or service and still there on the boat's return. As soon as the lifeboat was recovered, and pulled clear of the water, he would lift them into it for a short ride as it was pulled by the horses back into the boathouse. Most of the horses used for launching were kept in a field behind the Coastguard cottages opposite the lifeboat station, and apparently they preferred going to the beach than ploughing.

As for services undertaken, Proctor had to wait almost six years before her first effective service. During the morning of 10 January 1920 the 900-ton schooner Monte Grande, of Le Havre, which had been sailing in ballast from her home port to Haiti, was seen in difficulty about three miles off the entrance to Chichester Harbour. The vessel, dragging her anchors in very heavy seas and a west-south-westerly gale, had been caught out in bad weather in the Channel and was in need of immediate help.

Proctor launched at 10.50am, with the crew getting their boat through the heavy surf on the beach using the haul-off warp and afloat just twenty minutes after the maroons had been fired. Sail was set with one reef, but

▼ Dressed overall, Proctor leaves her carriage for a demonstration launch at the end of her naming ceremony on 9 June 1914. With her sails hoisted, she sailed level with the shore, with the children running along the beach trying to keep up with her. (By courtesy of Hayling Island RNLI)

▶ The survivors of the schooner Monte Grande on the remains of their wrecked vessel in January 1920. (By courtesy of Hayling Island RNLI)

halfway to the casualty conditions worsened necessitating further reefing by the lifeboat crew. Once on scene, the lifeboat was asked by the master to stand by, and this they did for nearly five hours. Two hawsers were passed between lifeboat and casualty, and the lifeboat rode astern while the crew waited for an improvement in the weather.

However, the schooner continued to drag her anchors as the bad weather did not abate, and she was getting dangerously close to the shore. Just as the daylight was fading, the crew of Monte Grande came on deck with their life belts on, and signalled that they wished to be taken off. The vessel was still afloat, so Coxswain Charlie Cole managed to take the lifeboat alongside with great difficulty, and as he did so the lifeboat was smashed against the ship several times. One of the lifeboatmen, G. Jones, injured his hand while lifeboat was alongside, and the boat itself was slightly damaged. However, all fifteen of the crew were rescued, jumping into the lifeboat together. One wave hit the lifeboat at this point, lifting and trapping her, temporarily, under the schooner's stern. But she fell away in the next trough, at which point Coxswain Cole found that the rudder had jammed and only with great difficulty was he able to free it.

▼ Proctor is hauled along the sea front on her launching carriage by a team of horses, ready to be launched from the beach. (From the Gordon Campbell Postcard Collection, held by the RNLI)

Great skill was then required on the part of Coxswain Cole as the heavily laden lifeboat, now with twenty-eight persons on board, made for Chichester Harbour with huge waves repeatedly sweeping over her. But the lifeboat and her occupants crossed the bar safely and landed the rescued men. They were billeted in an empty cottage, lent by Sir William Treloar, and Sister Wilkinson provided fuel and food for the night and breakfast. The lifeboat was manned during this service by Coxswain Charles Cole, Second Coxswain Ernie Cole, Bowman George Rowe, and crew members George Jones, Bob Goldring, Stephen Goldring, Bill Goldring, Bill Foster, Sam Gardner, Bill Burrows, Billy Miller, Peter Bowers and Thomas Raines.

Monte Grande was blown two miles further towards East Wittering during the night, and eventually became a total wreck, but her master later wrote a letter of thanks to Coxswain Cole and his crew. The letter was published in the local newspaper, and read as follows:

'TO THE CREW OF THE LIFEBOAT PROCTOR

'Dear Friends, I could not leave England without offering you my warmest thanks for the notable manner in which you hastened to our assistance. It was thanks to your efforts and in spite of the heavy seas running, that we were able to save the entire crew.

'Be sure that the men of the Monte Grande will ever remember the brave crew of the Proctor. Once more, thanking you all and with my best remembrance,

'L. Richard. Captain, wrecked ship Monte Grande.

'Chichester, 18 January 1920.'

▼ The 35ft Rubie self-righter Proctor, Hayling's last pulling lifeboat, being launched from the beach off her carriage. The Rubie self-righter, named after Felix Rubie, the RNLI's Chief Surveyor from 1906 to 1927, was a variation on the standard self-righter. The 35ft version, which was supplied to Hayling, was intended to be much better at sailing than the standard type as it had lower end boxes, and the water ballast tanks, which filled on launching, instead of an iron keel made it lighter to handle on a beach. (By courtesy of Hayling Island RNLI)

▶ A visit to the station by a group of Sea Scouts, who are pictured with Proctor in the lifeboat house in 1913 or 1914. (By courtesy of Hayling Island RNLI)

Six months later Proctor and her crew were involved in another fine service. On the morning of 20 June 1920 the 9,000-ton Government oil tanker Plumleaf was in collision with the British India Company's steamship Australia, off Portland, near Weymouth, in torrential rain, rough seas and a south-westerly wind. Australia was badly damaged, with several cabins smashed and other damage, which was fortunately above the water line. She had to put into Portland, but Plumleaf, which was on her way from Plymouth to Southampton, was able to proceed on her way. However, her compass had been damaged in the collision and, in the bad weather, with her Captain not being able to see any navigation lights, the vessel arrived off Chichester Harbour late on the Sunday afternoon, and went aground when about two miles south-east of the harbour entrance.

Proctor was launched at 5.35pm and when she arrived at the casualty, the master said he hoped to refloat his ship on the next high tide, so the lifeboatmen were asked to stand by the steamer. On board the casualty were sixty-two crew and six passengers, four women and two children. While the lifeboat stood by, several thousands of gallons of water ballast were pumped out of the vessel to lighten her, and between 2pm and 3pm Plumleaf refloated with the help of a tug. The Captain had asked the lifeboat, in the event of failure, to take the women and children ashore, but this was not needed. The bowman of the lifeboat, George Rowe, was a local pilot so he stayed aboard the vessel, which proceeded under tow to Southampton, while the lifeboat returned to station, where she arrived at 4am.

In heavy seas and gale force winds early on the afternoon of 26 September 1922 the small yacht Madge was seen about two miles south-east of Hayling Island Coastguard Station trying to reach harbour. But as Coxswain

Launching the Lifeboat. Hayling Island.

Charles Cole and his brother Ernie watched, the yacht first broached and then capsized as it was hit by the next wave. The crew was summoned and Proctor was launched at 1.05pm to go to the yacht's assistance. However, despite a thorough search, the lifeboatmen could find no trace of the missing yachtsmen. After nearly two hours the search was called off and the lifeboat returned to station. When nearing the beach she was struck by a huge breaking wave, which completely filled her, and some of the crew who had been in the boat for thirty years later said it was the heaviest sea they had ever experienced in returning to the shore. The yacht was later washed ashore near to Beachlands.

▼ Proctor on her launching carriage. She served at Hayling Island until 1924 and the station was closed when she was withdrawn. She was transferred to Berwick-on-Tweed where she served until 1930, launching nine more times on service and saving thirteen lives. (RNLI)

Closure of the station

Proctor on the beach, with her crew on board and station officials standing in front. She was the last pulling lifeboat to serve at Hayling. (RNLI)

The lifeboat house built in 1865 became a private residence until being extensively converted, and almost unrecognisable as a lifeboat house, in the late 1980s into the Inn on the Beach. (Nicholas Leach)

The last service launch by Proctor, and also the last by a pulling lifeboat at Hayling Island, took place on 26 August 1923 when a small yacht got into trouble. Soon after 5pm, a sharp-eyed Coastguard spotted the yacht Quick Step, of Hayling Island, with its top-mast carried away in very heavy seas and a strong south-westerly wind, three miles east of the Dean Tail Buoy and about six miles off Hayling Island. Coxswain Charles Cole went to the boathouse to consider the best course of action, and it was decided to telephone Bembridge lifeboat station as that lifeboat was to windward of the casualty. As she was a motor lifeboat, she would also be able to tow the yacht more easily.

The Bembridge motor lifeboat Langham launched at 6pm, but despite searching as far as east Selsey Bill could not find the yacht. When it was realised Langham had not found the yacht, Proctor was launched at 7.15pm into a heavy sea and strong spring tide, with Second Coxswain Ernie Cole in command. His brother, Charles, the Coxswain, was recovering from a serious illness and so was unable to go out. The lifeboat had a dead beat to windward, and when the Hayling boat covered a fair distance to the casualty, the Bembridge lifeboat apprached them and the crew informed the Bembridge crew of the yacht's exact location. The Bembridge boat soon reached the the yacht, which had one man on board, and rigged a tow. Proctor was recovered on the beach at

9.25pm, where 'the large crowd gave the crew a hearty cheer on their return', according to the Portsmouth Times.

By the 1920s the shipping pattern had changed and the smaller ports, such as Dell Quay, became less important as sail was overtaken by steam or motor. With motor lifeboats sent to the nearby stations of Selsey and Bembridge in 1922, the RNLI's Committee of Management decided, at its meeting on 15 May 1924, to close the station at Hayling. On Saturday 16 August 1924 Proctor was launched to give local residents who had supported the lifeboat a ride before she left. Proctor left Hayling Island on 29 September 1924 and was sailed to Saunder's yard at Cowes by Coxswain Charles Cole and his crew. She covered the ten miles to Ryde Pier in an hour, and reached Cowes in another hour. After a refit, she was sent to Berwick-on-Tweed.

With the closure of the Hayling Island station, Charles Cole, who had been Coxswain for the last five and a half years, and his borther Ernie Cole, Second Coxswain, were both granted pensions by the RNLI and presented with Certificates of Service. A Certificate was also awarded to George Jones, who had been on the crew for over twenty years and had not missed a service or exercise launch in that time. Charlie Cole had been just as dedicated, but owing to his illness on the last service, Jones gained one more launch.

The two lifeboat houses built at Hayling both survive. The first, built in 1865 when the station opened, was converted into a private residence, but was later heavily altered and became a public house, with little of the original building left. The house of 1914 remains essentially the same as it was when in use as a lifeboat house, and stands close to the new Coastguard station.

▼ The lifeboat house built in 1914 at a cost of £900 on the sea front, about two miles east of the first boathouse. The station closed in 1924 when it was used first as the village hall and then by the Army cadets. (Nicholas Leach)

The first inshore lifeboat

Afterthe last pulling lifeboat had been withdrawn, the seas off Hayling Island were covered by motor lifeboats at the nearby Bembridge and Selsey stations. The station had been closed in the 1920s in response to the changing pattern of casualties, and its reopening in the 1970s was in response to further such changes. During the late 1950s the number of inshore incidents to which lifeboats were being called increased as more people visited the coast for leisure activities. Many services were to bathers washed out to sea, children on lilos, dinghies, yachts and cabin cruisers.

Speed was vital in reaching the casualty before the situation deteriorated, and conventional motor lifeboats, none of which was capable of more than nine knots, were poorly suited to such work. A simple, fast rescue craft was required, so the RNLI bought an inflatable boat in 1962 for extensive trials, and a delegation visited France, where similar boats were in operation, to see them in service. Following these initial steps, the first inshore rescue boats, later inshore lifeboats (ILBs), were introduced during the summer of 1963 when eight were sent to stations around the country.

Such was their success that in each of the subsequent years more and more places began to operate the boats. In addition to the ILBs operated by the RNLI, a number of private inshore rescue boats were established at various places, one of which was Hayling Island. In 1966 Frank Martin and his two sons Guy and Leigh started a rescue patrol at Hayling using an inflatable boat, and they became part of the Shore Boat Rescue Scheme recognised by the RNLI. By 1966 they were using an old RNLI inflatable, number 007, which was powered by a 40hp Evinrude outboard. The boat was towed by an old

▼ The official opening of the station in August 1975, with the RNLI's old D class inflatable (on left), the HISRrO jet boat (centre) and the first Atlantic 21 B-511. The crews pictured are, with the first boat on left, Paul Covell, Tony Gardner, Paddy Lamperd, Ross Fuller, Clive Taylor, Graham Raines; with the second boat Simon Wilson, Paddy Newman, Mike Mountfield, Trevor Pearce plus one volunteer casualty; and with the third boat two divers, Brian Quintin, Frank Dunster, Albert Kirby and another crew member. (By courtesy of Hayling Island RNLI)

◀ The RNLI inflatable lifeboats were 16ft in length, made from nylon with neoprene, crewed by two, powered by a 40hp outboard engine, and could be launched quickly and easily. The HISRrO purchased an old inflatable from the RNLI and used it as a rescue boat off Hayling Island. The crew in the boat (on right) are, from left to right, Tony Graham, Simon Wilson and Frank Dunster. (By courtesy of Hayling Island RNLI)

Land Rover, and launched off the beach directly into the surf. A caravan next to the Coastguard station was used as a crew facility.

In 1971 Frank formalised the outfit by creating the Hayling Island Sea Rescue and Research Organisation (HISRrO), which not only provided a rescue service for the area with regular patrols along the local beaches, but also carried out research into rescue methods using divers. He designed and built a jet boat, using neoprene floats fashioned by the crew and mounted on a home-made rigid hull. The boat was powered by two Sunbeam Alpine marinised engines and could easily reach speeds in excess of thirty knots. The old RNLI inflatable remained in use alongside the jet boat.

Two years after this the HISRrO, having proved the need for an inshore lifeboat at Hayling, decided it would be beneficial to work with the RNLI. Discussions between the two organisations took place, and agreement was reached that the station would be operated jointly. With RNLI involvement, a double boathouse was built on a site leased from the Coldeast and Tatchbury Mount Croup Hospital Group at Sandy Point, on the eastern side of Hayling Island, and this was ready by early 1975.

The RNLI then sent an Atlantic 21, and intensive crew training with the new craft was undertaken. The Atlantic had been developed with the

◀ The locally-built rigid-inflatable jet boat, used for the HISRrO, being launched, with Simon Wilson, Graham Raines, Clive Taylor and Trevor Pearce as crew. (By courtesy of Hayling Island RNLI)

assistance of the Atlantic College in South Wales as a larger ILB capable of night operation, and with a greater range than the standard inshore lifeboat. The boat had a rigid wooden hull with an inflatable sponson attached and twin 40hp outboard engines to give a speed of over thirty knots. The design was ideally suited to the sea conditions off Hayling Island.

The first Atlantic 21 to serve the station was B-511, which was funded by members of the Co-operative Women's Guild of Great Britain and had been formally presented to the RNLI at a ceremony at Plymouth in September 1974 before coming to Hayling. One of her first services took place on 16 March 1975, before she had been officially placed on station. Helmsman Ross Fuller and crew members Simon Wilson and Paddy Lamperd had taken the boat out on a training exercise shortly before midday. As they proceeded to sea, they saw red flares being fired from the 16ft cabin cruiser Andrew John and altered course to help. The cruiser's engines were out of action, so a tow was secured and the disabled boat taken into Langstone Harbour.

After weeks of training, the RNLI placed Hayling Island lifeboat station on service on 25 March 1975. The first call came at 7.31pm on 30 March after Frank Martin received reports of an object falling into the sea about a mile and a half from the boathouse. With Tony Gardiner at the helm and Paddy Lamperd and Frank Dunster as crew, the ILB launched to investigate, but only found a large hot air balloon, which had broken from its tether. The lifeboatmen recovered the balloon and then returned to station.

The first life-saving service was performed on 10 May 1975 after a large number of dinghies had been caught out in rapidly deteriorating conditions during Hayling Island Sailing Club's National Solo Class race in the Bay, in which about seventy dinghies were involved. A violent squall capsized many of the dinghies and the Sailing Club rescue boats were unable to cope. The

▼ Crew and personnel outside the first ILB house at Sandy Point. (Supplied by Hayling Island RNLI)

◀ The lifeboat house built in 1974-5 for the station's first inshore lifeboats. The construction work was undertaken by Clive Taylor, a crew member who was also a builder, and whose son, Damien, later became one of the station's senior helmsman. (Nicholas Leach)

HISRrO rescue boat was called out, and B-511, which was already at sea on exercise with the RNLI's Divisional Inspector, also went to help. Many people were picked up and transferred to the Sailing Club's boats. B-511 was directed by Graham Raines in the HISRrO boat to a capsized dinghy with a man who had been in the water for over an hour. He had drifted nearly two miles and was hypothermic when rescued. After being given first aid on the ILB, he was rushed back to the boathouse for further treatment.

▲ The inshore lifeboat house built in 1974-5 with the launching ramp added in 1980. The beach constantly changes and this slipway is now completely buried by the shingle. (Nicholas Leach)

On 25 May 1975 lifeboats from many stations were called out as the weather was cold, wet and windy, with Hayling Island crew answering four calls in just ten hours. The first came at 11.45am, when B-511 launched to a sailing dinghy which had capsized off West Wittering. Another boat was able to help this casualty, but the lifeboatmen received a report that a yacht was in difficulty two miles offshore. The ILB found the auxiliary sloop Hapenny Breeze, which had been hit by another boat and holed. The hole was on the waterline so the lifeboat's swimmer went into the water to plug

it, after which the boat was towed to harbour. The next call came at 3.20pm, when the lifeboat went to the motor cruiser Our Oyster which was drifting off West Wittering in a force five north-easterly wind. The ILB reached the casualty to find its inexperienced crew had no anchor, distress flares or life-jackets and the boat's engine had broken. The boat was towed to harbour at 4.15pm. The fourth call of the day came at 9.30pm, when the lifeboat went to the yacht Dorothea, which was aground. The exhausted owner and his wife were rescued by the ILB, which went out again to tow in the yacht.

The official opening of the station was held on 2 August 1975. However, as the final preparations were being made, the ILB was called out on service at 9.40am, launching to the fishing boat My Lady, which had gearbox failure. The casualty was towed into Chichester Harbour and the ILB returned to station at 10.46am ready for the ceremony. With many people in attendance, the new lifeboat, named Co-operative No.1, was delivered into the care of the Hayling Island station by Vice-Admiral Sir Peter Compston, a member of the RNLI's Committee of Management. The joint RNLI/HISRrO inshore lifeboat station was officially declared open by Frank Judd MP, Under Secretary of State for Defence and the Navy, and, after a service of dedication, the lifeboat was launched for a short demonstration.

▼ Bob Berry and Roy Smith operate the launch and recovery winch used for the first inshore lifeboats at Hayling Island. (Supplied by Hayling Island RNLI)

The first year, 1975, was very busy for the nascent station and forty-four service launches were performed with thirty-five lives saved. During the following year, demand for the station's services was also high, with a particularly busy day on 15 May 1976. In near gale force south-westerly winds, creating rough seas, the motor vessel Swinging Safari

reported that a sailing dinghy had capsized near the Emsworth Channel, two miles from the station, and the dinghy's four occupants were in the water. The crews of the RNLI's ILB and HISRrO's inflatable were already at the boathouse when the message was received and B-511 launched at 2.13pm, reaching the casualty ten minutes later. The lifeboat's swimmer went into the water and helped the three children, all aged about twelve, and the man into the lifeboat.

The lifeboat then went to another capsized dinghy, to which the HISRrO inflatable was also launched. On the way to the second casualty, the crew of B-511 found that a boat from the Emsworth Sailing School, which had been towing in the first dinghy, was disabled with a rope round her propeller. The ILB's swimmer was able to clear the propeller and B-511 continued to the second dinghy. Three people were then spotted stranded on a sandbank and, as the Atlantic 21 could not get near enough to take them off, the HISRrO inflatable was diverted to help. The three were from a motor cruiser which had run aground and they got out to lighten the boat so that another boat could tow it off. They were left behind when the boat towing their craft kept going. The three people were landed at Itchenor, after which the HISRrO boat towed the abandoned dinghy to West Wittering Sailing Club.

The Coastguard then reported further casualties. A dismasted boat was in the vicinity of where the West Pole Beacon was later positioned, and another sailing dinghy had capsized off West Wittering and been swept out to sea. B-511 was sent to this casualty, while the HISRrO inflatable went to the other. The dinghy's crew of two were rescued by the Atlantic 21, which towed their

▼ A fine photograph of Hayling Island's first RNLI Atlantic 21, B-511, which served from 1975 to 1979 and saved almost 100 lives in that time. (By courtesy of Hayling Island RNLI)

boat back to Hayling Island Sailing Club, and the HISRrO inflatable escorted the other casualty, the motor cruiser Merry Dancer, safely into harbour. The rescue craft returned to station after three testing hours at sea.

A fine service was undertaken on 14 October 1976 after a yacht got into difficulty south-east of Chichester Harbour, and was dragged west by force seven winds, which built to force ten during the service. B-511 launched to help at 11.17am and encountered very heavy seas as she battled to reach the yacht, the 36ft sloop Sundew. Broadside to the seas, she was being swamped by large waves. Once the ILB reached the casualty, she was manoeuvred alongside and one of the crew boarded the yacht, finding three people huddled in the water-logged cabin. The yacht bounced over the East Winner on her beam ends and then a line was secured, but the heavy seas made the tow very difficult. Eventually the boats reached Langstone Marina and the yachtsmen were landed. For this service, Letters of Appreciation signed by the RNLI Director, Captain Nigel Dixon, were sent to Helmsman Paddy Lamperd, and crew Nicholas Danby, Simon Wilson, and Paul Covell.

Another long and difficult service was undertaken on 3 January 1978 when B-511 was called out after a fishing boat was reported overdue. Unusual weather had created shingle banks on the beach at the launch site, and it took eight shore helpers and three attempts to launch the ILB. It was bitterly cold and the Honorary Medical Adviser Dr Richard Newman was taken in case the anglers were suffering from hypothermia. At 3.54am the ILB headed for the Emsworth Channel in a near gale force westerly wind and eleven minutes later the crew spotted the cabin cruiser Tomey Too hard aground off Thorney Island. A boy from the casualty was taken onto the ILB,

▼ B-525 outside the lifeboat house at Hayling Island with crew members, from left to right, Graham Raines, Robert Berry, Frank Dunster, Roy Smith and Rod James, and Bella, the lifeboat dog. (Supplied by Hayling Island RNLI)

◄ The second Atlantic 21 to serve at Hayling Island, B-525, with four crew members on board. (By courtesy of Hayling Island RNLI)

and efforts were made to pull the cabin cruiser clear. This proved impossible, so she was anchored and the owner taken aboard the ILB. With the gale still blowing, the Atlantic 21 grounded on the mud, and the crew had to go into the water to push her clear. This was extremely difficult, with the crew in water two feet deep one minute, but up to their necks in freezing water the next. Crew member Frank Dunster took an anchor towards the deeper channel and using this the ILB was eventually pulled clear. For this long and difficult service, Framed Letters of Thanks, signed by the Chairman of the RNLI Major-General Ralph Farrant, were later presented to Helmsman Paddy Lamperd and crew members Frank Dunster, Brian Quinton and Dr Newman. A Letter of Thanks, signed by the RNLI's Director Captain Nigel Dixon, was sent to the launching personnel, in appreciation of their considerable efforts.

In March 1978 the RNLI and HISRrO agreed to discontinue their joint association and the RNLI became solely responsible for the station at Sandy Point, which was operated along the same lines as its other stations. Frank Martin, Chairman of HISRrO and also a Vice-Chairman of the newly formed Solent Safety Organisation, resigned and was replaced as Honorary Secretary by Roy Smith, while HISRrO continued its rescue and research work.

What proved to be the last service launch by B-511 at Hayling Island took place on 22 October 1979 when she towed the cabin cruiser Nerissa 2, with three people on board, off a mud bank in the Bosham Channel. In just four and a half years at Hayling Island, B-511 launched 170 times and saved ninety-eight lives. She was replaced in October 1979 by another Atlantic 21, B-525, a relief boat, which served for just over a year. B-525 completed a number of routine rescues, with her first effective service coming on 11 November 1979, when she went to the fishing vessel Kathy. Several attempts to tow the boat out of very heavy surf in Bracklesham Bay and to sea failed, but the all-weather lifeboat from Selsey subsequently took the disabled fishing boat in tow to Chichester Harbour and the Atlantic 21 returned to station.

Aldershot

▶ B-548 Aldershot is readied for launching at the end of her formal naming ceremony at Hayling Island on 4 July 1981. Unusually, crew members of the Cromer lifeboat were present because some of the funds for the new Atlantic 21 came from monies left over from the Cromer Lifeboat Appeal. (By courtesy of Hayling Island RNLI)

In November 1980 a new Atlantic 21, number B-548, was placed on station at Hayling Island. The boat had been built for the station, unlike the previous Atlantics which were both second-hand, and served the station for almost fourteen years. Costing £25,000, she was funded by the Aldershot Branch and a legacy from Doris Marjorie Chartres, and was named Aldershot. The formal naming ceremony was held on 4 July 1981, when the new boat was handed over by Lt Cdr J. J. Town-Clear, RNR, Chairman of the Aldershot Branch. The boat was dedicated by the Vicar of Hayling Island, the Rev Nigel O'Connor, after which she was launched for a demonstration.

During her career at Hayling Island, Aldershot was used for some very fine services. Indeed, by the time of her inauguration she had been involved in an outstanding rescue. On 14 December 1980, just a month after the new boat arrived, she was called to the yacht Fitz's Flyer, which was in difficulty off Eastoke Point and was being driven towards the shore in a force eight westerly gale. DLA Sir David Mackworth, realising the urgency of the situation, authorised an immediate launch and B-548 Aldershot set off at 1.20pm with Frank Dunster as Acting Helmsman, and Trevor Pearce and sixteen-year-old Graham Wickham as crew. The ILB faced very heavy seas with waves up to 6ft high, and conditions at the bar were particularly bad. The ILB's speed had to be reduced to about eight knots and Acting Helmsman Dunster had to use the throttles to minimise the impact of the seas. Just as the yacht was sighted about 400 yards away, the ILB was hit by a large wave, which completely engulfed and almost capsized her. She fell heavily into the trough and both engines stalled, but they were quickly restarted.

When the ILB was only a few yards from the yacht, another very heavy sea hit her, she fell heavily into the trough, and both engines stalled again, but were restarted imediately. A second run was made, again without success, but on the third attempt two of the yacht's crew were rescued. Four more runs had to be made before the third yachtsman was rescued. On the next approach the last member of the yacht's crew was rescued and taken aboard the ILB. The lifeboat reached Hayling Island Sailing Club at 1.50pm, and the survivors were landed. For this excellent service, demanding great courage and fine seamanship, Acting Helmsman Frank Dunster was awarded the Bronze medal by the RNLI. For their part, the Institution's Thanks on Vellum was awarded to crew-members Trevor Pearce and Graham Wickham.

Nine months after this outstanding service, B-548 Aldershot was involved in a series of rescues on 19 September 1981 after a variety of sea-users got into difficulties in gale-force south-easterly winds and heavy rain squalls. The first call came at 4pm when B-548 Aldershot launched, with Frank Dunster at the helm and Rod James and Graham Raines as crew, to pick up a windsurfer, who was totally exhausted in the strong winds. Just as he was being put ashore, another windsurfer was seen in difficulties in the Emsworth Channel, so the ILB rescued him. The lifeboat then went to investigate reports that a dinghy had capsized close to the Hayling Island Bridge, but the dinghy and her crew were safe so the lifeboat returned down the Emsworth Channel.

By now, the wind had risen to force nine. An 18ft yacht, which had been blown ashore just north of the Verner Beacon was the next casualty, and having rigged a tow to the yacht, the ILB was asked to urgently help a person clinging to a groyne off Sandy Point. The tow was slipped and the yacht's crew dropped anchor so the ILB could head for Sandy Point at full speed.

▼ Atlantic 21 B-548 Aldershot puts out towards the surf line. (By courtesy of Hayling Island RNLI)

To reach the casualty Helmsman Dunster took the ILB across the West Pole Sands through very heavy, confused seas, which caused the ILB to be almost vertical at times. The lifeboatmen saw the trapped person, a teenage boy, about twenty yards from the seawall, clinging desperately to the groyne, and engulfed by heavy seas rebounding off the seawall. Shore helper Trevor Pearce attempted to reach him from the seawall, helped by Bill Langford, but the heavy seas proved too much.

Helmsman Dunster took the Atlantic 21 to the east side of the groyne, to get to the trapped boy. But the ILB was caught by a large wave and broached, which stalled both engines. They were restarted, but the ILB was then hit by another huge wave, turned broadside and pushed onto her sponson. She came upright again, only to be hit by the same wave rebounding off the seawall. The ILB was taken into deeper water and approached the groyne stern first, but the backwash of waves off the seawall made this manoeuvre impossible so another attempt was made bow first. On this attempt the ILB was picked up by a large, curling wave and lifted over the groyne.

An approach was then made from the western side of the groyne, but both engines stalled in the heavy seas. They were restarted and the ILB had to be taken full astern to avoid being smashed into the seawall. Once clear of the surf Helmsman Dunster and his two crew agreed that the ILB could not get close enough to rescue the boy, so it was agreed that the boat would get as close as possible and then one of the crew would go into the water and try to swim over to the boy. As they were preparing to bring the ILB in towards the groyne, another attempt was made to reach the boy from the shore. Shore helper Nigel Roper, wearing a dry suit with a line tied round his waist, went into the water to try and reach the boy. But he was unable to make any headway in the heavy seas and was caught by the pounding surf and flung against the seawall, and fortunately was uninjured by the attempt.

▼ Atlantic 21 B-548 Aldershot launching down the ramp at Sandy Point. (By courtesy of Hayling Island RNLI)

◄ Atlantic 21 B-548 Aldershot on service to the sand dredger FPT 1V on 18 March 1989 in south-westerly force eight winds. Despite the challenging conditions, B-548 reached the casualty, which had developed a severe list, and took off the three crew. Sixty seconds later the dredger capsized. B-548 made a slow and cautious return across the bar as the conditions worsened. This picture was painted by local marine artist Rex Phillips (an ex-Naval Commander) and a copy was presented by Brian Read to HRH The Princess Royal at Hayling Island Sailing Club. (By courtesy of Hayling Island RNLI)

Helmsman Dunster took the ILB as close to the boy as he could and Rod James entered the water to swim to the boy. But when he was 10ft from the boy, James saw him let go and disappear beneath the waves. After several seconds the boy reappeared, about 6ft away. James reached him to find him unconscious, turned him onto his back and began swimming for the shore, where both were pulled to safety by Nigel Roper and Trevor Pearce. James managed to lift the boy up to Bill Langford, who pulled him onto the seawall and to safety. The boy was suffering from hypothermia and had cuts to his body, so was immediately taken to hospital by ambulance.

With crew member Rod James and the boy safely ashore at 5.45pm, Helmsman Dunster set off back to the lifeboat station. But five minutes later the lifeboatmen spotted a 30ft cabin cruiser heading towards the West Pole Sands, so Helmsman Dunster warned the owner, and then escorted the craft into harbour. At 6pm Rod James rejoined the Atlantic 21 at the boathouse and the windsurfer, who had been on board throughout the attempts to rescue the boy, was finally landed. The ILB then went back to the yacht and found that its anchor had not held and it had gone aground. As the ILB went alongside to pass a line, she too went aground, and the lifeboatmen entered the water and pulled both boats clear before rigging a tow.

Off Mill Rythe, the tow parted in 8ft waves and therefore a second line was secured and they got under way again at 6.27pm, just as another yacht was seen in difficulties on the nearby Pilsey Sands. When the first yacht had been secured to a buoy, the ILB went to the second yacht, which had been blown onto the sands. As he grasped the yacht's handrails, Rod James was thrown out of the ILB by the rough seas, and had to be pulled back on board by Graham Raines, after which the four people on the yacht were saved.

The ILB returned to the other yacht, which was taken to a safer mooring and her two crew taken off. All six people were landed at the boathouse at 7pm, but ten minutes later yet another call was received. With two extra

▶ Frank Dunster, one of the original crew and medal-winning helmsman. (By courtesy of the RNLI)

crew on board, the ILB was launched, going to a catamaran in trouble off Pilsey Island and then being diverted to a trimaran off the Hayling Island Sailing Club. The crews from these vessels were taken aboard the ILB and landed at the Sailing Club, with the ILB finally being rehoused at 8pm.

In recognition of this remarkable series of services, and for his courage, superb seamanship and outstanding leadership, Frank Dunster was awarded his second Bronze medal. For his part, and particularly for the rescue of the boy on the groyne, the RNLI awarded the Silver medal to Rod James. Crew member Graham Raines was accorded the Thanks of the Institution Inscribed on Vellum, as were shore helpers Trevor Pearce and Nigel Roper.

On 5 June 1983 the Hayling Island lifeboat had an extremely busy day. The first call was just after lunch to a young boy drifting out to sea in a rubber boat. B-548 brought the boy back to shore and then went to stand by a fleet of sailing dinghies, with the lifeboatmen assisting a number of boats which capsized when a storm hit the area. At 2.55pm B-548 went to the yacht Chippawa, which was in difficulty off the Chichester Bar Beacon. A launch from the Itchenor Sailing Club took the casualty in tow, and both boats were escorted by the ILB. The ILB also helped a surfboarder in difficulties south-east of Eastoke Point, and then rescued a boy who was being blown out to sea in an inflatable canoe. The next casualty was the yacht Optica, which was in trouble off the Chichester Bar. Battling rough seas on the Bar, the ILB's crew secured a line, with difficulty, and towed the yacht to safety.

Two sailboarders in trouble near the East Pole Sands were helped next, and they were landed on West Wittering beach. The lifeboatmen then spotted two more sailboarders needing assistance, and they too were rescued and landed on the beach, while another surfboarder was picked up by the ILB as the lifeboat crew were giving further help to Optica. The yacht Hideaway was next in need of help, but she refloated unaided. After another two sailboarders were helped, the ILB was directed to a yacht, which had run aground 200 yards south of the station. Helmsman Lamperd waded to the casualty with a line, which was passed to the fishing boat North Star, and the yacht was pulled clear and towed to Hayling Island Sailing Club. Following these services, the RNLI's Chief of Operations sent a Letter of Appreciation to Honorary Secretary Roy Smith thanking everyone involved, with particular mention of the part played by Paddy Lamperd in swimming out to North Star with the line from the grounded yacht.

Although the Hayling lifeboats largely perform routine services, a noteworthy service was undertaken on 7 December 1986. B-548 Aldershot was launched after a red flare had been seen in Bracklesham Bay. The force six southerly wind and rough seas made crossing the Bar very difficult, but once clear Helmsman Frank Dunster altered course and crossed the East Pole Sands towards the casualty, with the ILB encountering large waves during the passage. As they cleared the sands, the lifeboatmen saw an angling boat close to the shoal area so the ILB went alongside and crew member David Sigournay jumped across. The boat's single occupant was badly bruised and, as he was not wearing a life jacket, Sigournay put his own life jacket on him. He then manoeuvred the angling boat clear, although in the rough seas the small boat rolled heavily, and broached three times after being hit by large following seas, being pushed over so far it was feared she would capsize.

The injured man was in severe shock, but Helmsman Dunster decided it would be impractical to transfer him to the ILB so they carried on, with the ILB remaining close by the casualty. The boats crossed the bar safely and by 10.50am the angling boat had been placed on moorings, with the injured man transferred to an ambulance. For his expert seamanship and courage during this service, David Sigournay was accorded the Thanks Inscribed on Vellum by the RNLI, with Vellum Service Certificates presented to Frank Dunster and Jonathan Bradbury.

◀ Six of Hayling Island's lifeboat crew from the 1980s. Back, left to right, Warren Hayes, Rod James, and Chris Reed; front, left to right, Damien Taylor, Evan Lamperd and Frank Dunster. (By courtesy of the RNLI)

During the early afternoon of 24 September 1988 B-548 Aldershot was launched to help the ketch Seaway Endeavour, which was in difficulties with a jammed rudder and stalled engine. With Helmsman Rod James in command, the lifeboat found the ketch drifting in very rough seas and a near gale force wind on the East Pole Sands, about to became engulfed by seas on the sandbank. But on the approach, the lifeboat was struck by two large breaking waves, broached, and was completely engulfed before Rod James could bring her back under control.

At this point, Frank Dunster arrived on scene in the 28ft rigid-inflatable boat Hayling Rescue with Chris Driscoll as crew. He realised that the ketch was in dangerously shallow water, and so he and Rod James agreed to take the crew off the ketch as quickly as possible. Frank took his boat towards the ketch and, with great skill, held her alongside. The boat remained alongside while five people were rescued, and the heavy seas then swept the inflatable away and Rod James took the Atlantic 21 to the casualty.

The Atlantic was knocked away initially, but on a second run one person was rescued, while another fell into the sea. He was quickly picked up and the Atlantic was brought round for another run. Three more attempts were needed to save the remaining two people from the ketch. The two inflatables then returned to harbour where the nine survivors were landed. For their skill, courage and fine seamanship during this rescue, Framed Letters of Thanks signed by the Chairman of the RNLI, His Grace The Duke of Atholl, were presented to Rod James and Frank Dunster.

Another fine rescue was performed on 9 October 1988 after the 32ft yacht Dingaling got into difficulty as she approached Chichester Harbour in very rough seas and a near gale force south-westerly wind. The yacht was knocked over by the heavy seas, and two of the nine crew were swept overboard. The remaining crew put out a mayday and at 1.17pm Portsmouth's Atlantic 21 B-550 City of Portsmouth set off to help, while the relief ILB at Hayling Island, B-526, was launched three minutes later. At 1.25pm the Hayling Island lifeboat approached the casualty and Helmsman Frank Dunster spotted a man in the water, so manoeuvred the ILB towards him. Crew member Graham Raines jumped into the sea, swam to the man and, inflating his own life jacket, supported him. The helicopter, which was also on scene, had spotted the other person who had been swept overboard from the yacht, and picked her up, but sadly she was found to be dead.

The man helped by Graham Raines was alive, but as crew member Rod James leaned over to help the two men into the ILB, the motion of the boat threw him overboard, leaving Helmsman Dunster on the ILB. Portsmouth's Atlantic arrived on scene at this point, and with great skill Helmsman Martin Icke took her alongside and crew member Paul Venton jumped across. He pulled the yachtsman and Raines aboard the Hayling boat, and Rod James hauled himself back aboard. The barely conscious yachtsman was given first aid by Rod Janes, but an extremely heavy sea struck the boat at one

◄ Three photos of Atlantic 21 B-548 being launched on her trolley across the beach and setting out on exercise. (By courtesy of Hayling Island RNLI)

point, carrying the survivor between the engines. As the lifeboat came clear, the starboard engine stopped. However, she continued on one engine into sheltered waters so that the yachtsman could be lifted off by helicopter.

Paul Venton transferred back to the Portsmouth ILB which, with the Hayling Island boat, escorted Dingaling into the harbour. For their skill and courage during this demanding service, crew member Graham Raines was awarded the Bronze medal by the RNLI. The Thanks Inscribed on Vellum was accorded to Frank Dunster and Rod James, and to the Portsmouth crew of Martin Icke, Paul Venton and Adrian West.

Incredibly, this medal-winning rescue was not the last undertaken in B-548 Aldershot, as another extraordinary rescue was performed in her on 25 October 1992. The 75ft ketch Donald Searle, with seventeen people on board, got into difficulty at the eastern end of Chichester Bar in a fifty-knot westerly gale. Her engines had failed and she was dragging her anchor in 15ft to 20ft breaking seas. But B-548 Aldershot was already on service, so helmsman Frank Dunster, on hearing the Mayday sent by the ketch, put out in his own 28ft single-engined rigid-inflatable, Hayling Rescue, with two lifeboat volunteers, Evan Lamperd and Damien Taylor as crew.

As Hayling Rescue crossed the huge waves on the Bar, Dunster saw the ketch in shallow water and in great danger. He approached Donald Searle, and on the second attempt came alongside to take off the first of the yacht's crew. Staying alongside was extremely difficult as the seas threatened to smash Hayling Rescue against the casualty, but in spite of this Dunster continued his efforts and took off another person. He was increasingly concerned for the safety of his own boat, as avoiding a capsize was taking all his boathandling skill, and so he headed for the calmer waters of Chichester

▼ Atlantic 21 B-548 Aldershot flies off a wave. On board are Graham Raines, Damien Taylor and Jonathan Bradbury. (By courtesy of Hayling Island RNLI)

Harbour. With five people aboard, his boat was difficult to handle, but he landed the two survivors at the lifeboat station at 12.35pm .

Meanwhile, B-548 Aldershot was making her way towards Donald Searle through the 20ft seas, one of which was so steep that it stood the lifeboat on end and Helmsman James thought she was about to capsize bow over stern. Both engines stalled but they were restarted, and the Atlantic reached the casualty. Helmsman James then began a series of approaches, and five times put the lifeboat's sponson alongside the ketch, breaking away each time to avoid being crushed by the casualty as she rose and fell in the heavy swell. After the five approaches five people had been taken off. On the next approach crew member Christopher Reed went aboard the casualty, while two more survivors jumped into the lifeboat.

A helicopter had arrived on scene by this time, and Reed took the line so that the helicopter winchman could get aboard the ketch, despite the casualty's violent motion. The lifeboat then returned to station with seven survivors, leaving the helicopter to winch off the remaining eight people. By 12.42pm Bembridge's 47ft Tyne lifeboat was on scene to help in the evacuation, and although she pulled off a survivor, when she hit the yacht both vessels were damaged and so the Coxswain decided it would be safer to stand off and allow the helicopter to continue winching. By 12.52pm the mission was accomplished, with all seven remaining yacht crew, lifeboat crew Christopher Reed and the winchman safely aboard the helicopter.

Following this rescue, Rod James and Frank Dunster were awarded the Silver medal, while the Thanks Inscribed on Vellum was accorded to the crews of both the Hayling Island lifeboat and Hayling Rescue. James became the first ILB helmsman to be awarded a second Silver medal. In his official report, Deputy Divisional Inspector Colin Williams wrote of Helmsman Roderick James: 'The fact that the Atlantic 21 did not founder in the steep breaking seas was doubtless due to his considerable skill and boat handling.' This was the last of the outstanding rescues undertaken in the Atlantic 21, which had proved herself to be a remarkable craft.

Station upgraded

▶ A dramatic photograph of B-712 Betty Battle, the Atlantic 75 which served at Hayling Island from 1995 to 2009. The Atlantic 75 was 24ft by 8ft 8in in size, larger than the boat she replaced, and was powered by twin 70hp outboards. These gave her a speed of over thirty knots, making her the fastest type in the RNLI's fleet. (By courtesy of the RNLI)

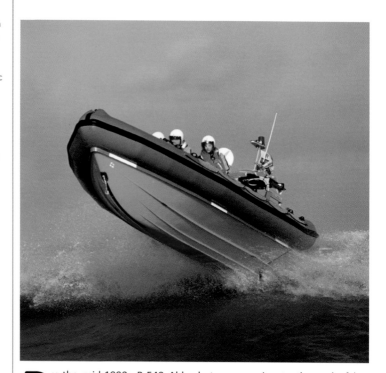

By the mid-1990s B-548 Aldershot was coming to the end of her operational life, and so one of the next generation of Atlantic class lifeboats, an Atlantic 75, was allocated to Hayling Island. A 16ft D class inflatable lifeboat was also supplied to the station to deal with casualties close to the shore and to provide back up to the Atlantic. B-548 Aldershot left the station on 6 October 1994, and was replaced temporarily by the relief Atlantic 21 B-541 Elizabeth Bestwick, which had been built in 1976 and funded from the bequest of Miss E. A. Bestwick. She stayed until 11 January 1995, when she was replaced by another relief Atlantic 21, B-526, which had served at Harwich for almost a decade and came to Hayling for six months until the new Atlantic 75 was ready for service.

To house two boats and provide better facilities for the volunteer crew, a new lifeboat station was built on the site of the 1970s house, which was demolished. The Atlantic was berthed at Sparkes Marina during the thirteen months of reconstruction. The new house provided much improved crew and training facilities, a workshop, drying and changing rooms and a small museum-cum-display area, and was funded by a local appeal. Over 8,000 appeal letters were sent to the boat owners of Chichester Harbour, as a

◀ The lifeboat house built in 1994-5 to house both Atlantic 75 and D class inflatable inshore lifeboats. (Nicholas Leach)

result of which more than £24,000 was donated. The remainder was raised by other events, such as auctions and coffee mornings. Over £115,000 was collected to pay for the new building, which was completed in 1995.

The new Atlantic 75, B-712 Betty Battle, was placed on station on 21 June 1995. The 75 was larger and more powerful than the Atlantic 21, and the prototype of the design, B-700, had been on trials at Hayling Island in January 1995 for a few days to assess its suitability to the area. B-700, which was funded by Susan and Michael Peacock of Itchenor, who were strong supporters of Hayling Island station, undertook three services during the trials, saving two sailboarders and bringing in a yacht and its four occupants in the space of a week. The station's own Atlantic 75, B-712, was called into action for the first time on 24 June, three days after arriving, going to a yacht and then a sailboarder, but help was not needed.

The first effective service by B-712 came on 28 June 1995, when she launched at 11pm to the yacht Avro and its three crew, who were stranded off the entrance to Chichester Harbour. The Atlantic 75 waited three quarters of an hour after launching before the vessel was floated off on the rising tide. The yacht's three crew were unable to get the craft off the bank, so crew member Roy Woods had to go into the water to free the anchor, but then the yacht's engine would not start and the crew were unsure of their position. So B-712 took the vessel in tow, found the owner's mooring off Dell Quay, and the ILB crew carried the two elderly gentlemen ashore.

▼ The scene at Hayling Island during the naming of the Atlantic 75 B-712 Betty Battle on 19 September 1995. (By courtesy of Hayling Island RNLI)

By the time B-712 was on station, a D class inflatable had been sent to Hayling Island. The first D class was D-398 Victory Wheelers, from the Relief Fleet, which went on

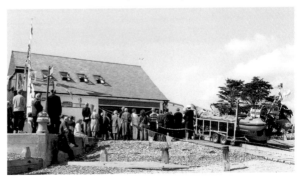

▶ Dr Graham Lowe, Chairman of the Appeal, unveils the commemorative plaque to formally open the new lifeboat house on 19 September 1995. (By courtesy of Hayling Island RNLI)

station on 23 March 1995, ready for the summer season, and initially for evaluation trials to assess the suitability of a D class ILB at Hayling Island. She stayed for almost exactly a year, before being replaced on 12 March 1996 by the new ILB D-496 Leonard Stedman.

The opening and dedication of the new boathouse and the naming of B-712 Betty Battle took place on 19 September 1995, almost exactly 130 years to the day since the station was first opened and the first lifeboat, Olive Leaf, was named. The new boathouse was opened by David Sandeman, whose great grandfather had hosted the opening in 1865, and who unveiled the commemorative plaque. Also in attendance were descendants of the station's past coxswains, crews and donors of lifeboats, together with the great grandson of Major Festing, who had led the rescue of the brig Ocean in 1865. Michael Woodroffe, Deputy Chief of Operations accepted the lifeboat on behalf of the RNLI, and formally handed her into the care of Brian Read, the Honorary Secretary. The service of dedication was conducted by the Rev Patrick McManus, and Mrs Betty Battle officially named the lifeboat.

After D-398 had spent the summer of 1995 proving that a D class inflatable was a useful addition to the station's capabilities, a new D class was allocated to the station. The new boat, D-496 Leonard Stedman, was funded by the Farnham Branch and named at a ceremony on 15 June 1996, similar in format to the Atlantic 75 ceremony the previous year. During the ceremony the boat was handed over by Rear Admiral Michael Stacey, CBE, President of the Farnham Branch and a member of the RNLI's Committee of Management, and was accepted by Michael Woodroffe. He, in turn, handed the boat into the care of Brian Read, and a service of dedication was conducted by the Rev Patrick McManus. At the end of the ceremony, Mrs Lois Stedman, widow of Leonard Stedman, named the boat which was then launched.

▶ B-712 Betty Battle launching on exercise on 31 July 1996 before the launching tractor had been sent to the station. The trolley was run down the beach by hand, and the boat floated off stern first. (Nicholas Leach)

◄ The D class inflatable D-398 Victory Wheelers, outside the lifeboat house in May 1995, was the first ILB to serve at Hayling Island. Coincidentally, D-398 was funded by the Victory Wheelers Custom Car Club, which used to meet on Hayling Island, and was a relief boat. She served at Hayling until March 1996, when a new ILB had been built for the station. (Nicholas Leach)

◄ The D class inflatable D-496 Leonard Stedman on exercise off Sandy Point. Funded by the Farnham Branch of the RNLI, she was named after the Branch's founder, and served at Hayling Island for nine years. (Nicholas Leach)

Four days after the ceremony, on 19 June 1996, as the crew was mustering for a Wednesday evening exercise, a power boat was seen to strand herself on the highest part of the Winner Bank in Chichester Harbour. As the lifeboats were about to launch on exercise, the helmsman went to check the casualty. The Atlantic 75 was taken alongside and found five persons on board, but as it would be some hours before the vessel could be refloated, the helmsman decided to take the four women off and return them to Chichester Marina. The skipper was left on board, as the damaged engine was still able to provide propulsion, and the vessel refloated on the next tide.

A rapid launch was necessary on 12 October 1997 after a man got into difficulties following the capsize of his dinghy. B-712 Betty Battle proceeded to the Emsworth Channel and, with the aid of the searchlight and light intensifier, the fifty-nine-year-old casualty was quickly located. He was taken on board and given first aid for hypothermia, while an ambulance was requested to meet the lifeboat at Emsworth Quay. At the quay, the casualty

► D class inflatable D-496 Leonard Stedman served at Hayling Island from 1996 to 2005. (Nicholas Leach)

showed signs of shock, but he was kept warm and reassured, and was passed into the care of the ambulance as soon as it arrived. B-712 was then tasked with locating the dinghy, which was found close to the casualty's original location and towed, semi waterlogged, to Emsworth Quay.

The D class inflatable D-496 Leonard Stedman was called into action on 6 August 1998, putting out at 5pm to help two children stuck in the mud between Emsworth and Fowley Island. The crew of D-496 located the two children, with one up to her waist in mud and the other up to her chest. The ILB was taken as close as possible before two crew, with mud pattens on, walked to the girls who were extricated and taken back to the lifeboat. The ILB helmsman was concerned about the condition of one of the girls and so requested a helicopter, which took the casualties to Haslar Hospital in

▼ Atlantic 75 B-712 Betty Battle on exercise, crewed by Andy Ellender, Ian Harris and Peter Hanscombe. (Nicholas Leach)

◀ Relief Atlantic 75 B-736 Toshiba Wave Warrior and D class inflatable D-496 Leonard Stedman launching on exercise. The tractors were introduced in 1998, with Talus MB764 TW43 used to launch the Atlantic and the Ford 6640 tractor TA38 supplied for launching the D class. Squeezing the launch vehicles into the existing boathouse was very difficult, and the Ford tractor had to be kept outside. The lack of space for the tractors was one of the reasons the boathouse was extensively rebuilt in 2007. (Nicholas Leach)

◀ Relief Atlantic 75 B-736 Toshiba Wave Warrior on exercise off Hayling Ialand in August 1999. B-736 was at Hayling Island from June 1999 to 31 January 2000 while B-712 was taken to the Inshore Lifeboat Centre at Cowes to be refitted. (Nicholas Leach)

Gosport. The rescue of the casualties from a life-threatening position over 1,000ft from shore reflected good team work by all involved.

On 31 July 1999 B-712 Betty Battle made a goodwill visit to Emsworth, after which she proceeded to Langstone to attend the annual raft race by the Ship Inn. An unplanned change of route for the race led to the rafts getting caught in the tidal flow which races under the bridge joining Hayling to the mainland, and a number of rafts got into difficulty. The Atlantic 75 arrived on scene just after the race had started, with many of the homemade rafts breaking up when they hit the supports of the bridge. The competitors were thrown into the water and swept into Langstone harbour. The lifeboat crew immediately started to help individuals from the water and return them to the quay, while another craft manned by one of the senior helmsmen also helped. In total three rafts were brought ashore along with many people.

Later during 1999 the relief Atlantic 75 B-736 Toshiba Wave Warrior was on station and on 24 October 1999 she was involved in a very challenging

► The view from the helicopter of Atlantic 75 B-712 Betty Battle during a lifting execise. (By courtesy of Hayling Island RNLI)

service. She was just returning from exercise when she was tasked to a boat in difficulty at Emsworth. B-736 immediately set off and found the casualty on the sea wall adjacent to the Tarquin Yacht Harbour. The vessel had been drifting downwind and was now being washed up alongside the rough cast concrete sea wall. During the initial attempts to get close, the lifeboat was swept onto the sea wall and grounded, causing the port engine to stop. But it was quickly restarted and the lifeboat crew managed to get a towline aboard. The casualty was then towed to deeper water, and placed on a mooring.

On 21 December 2002 both Hayling lifeboats were launched in foggy conditions after an angling boat had been reported overdue. B-712 Betty Battle searched from Bullock Patch northwards, and the D class searched the sandbanks south of Hayling Island, while Bembridge all-weather lifeboat and the Coastguard helicopter were also tasked. After an hour, the D class found the casualty south of Gunner Point, close to the entrance to Langstone Harbour. They had become disorientated in the fog so the ILB stood by and managed to refloat the angling boat, and then escorted her to safety.

In a fresh breeze on 6 September 2003 B-712 Betty Battle rescued ten people and a dog from a rigid-inflatable which was in danger of sinking in choppy seas three miles south of the entrance to Chichester Harbour. The boat had four adults, five teenagers, a child and a dog on board when the engine failed just after 5pm. The vessel had started to take on water and was soon awash, and two of the female passengers were suffering from seasickness. Betty Battle was soon on scene and took off seven of the people and the dog, and towed the casualty into Chichester Harbour. Three persons stayed on the RIB attempting to bail it out whilst under tow.

An unusual rescue was undertaken on 16 July 2004 after four horses, saddled but without riders, were spotted on the East Winner Bank off the west end of Hayling Island. B-712 Betty Battle was launched at 9pm, followed soon after by the D-496 Leonard Stedman as the horses were stranded on the East Winner Bank in a rising tide and the D class inflatable was required. The lifeboat crew, using flares and the fire brigade's thermal imaging equipment, found the horses, whose riders were safely ashore, and

◀ On 5 June 2004 trials with one of the RNLI's hovercraft were undertaken at Hayling Island. (By courtesy of Hayling Island RNLI)

guided two to the shore. A third was towed by the D class inflatable back to safety, where a veterinary surgeon was waiting to check the condition of the animals. Unfortunately one did not survive, but the horse that was towed to the shore was saved by crew member Paul Lewis, who entered the water, inflated his life jacket and put his body under the horses head. The horse riders were unaware of the dangers of the tide racing over the East Winner Bank and had got cut off by the tide, -which turns the Bank into an island.

The lifeboat crews were on service for three hours to help the stranded animals, and as a result of their efforts they were awarded with a Certificate of Merit by the Royal Society for the Prevention of Cruelty to Animals. The Certificate was presented on 8 February 2004 by Chief Inspector Paul Williams from the RSPCA in the presence of the Mayor of Havant Council, Councillor Mrs Hilary Farrow, and Mayoress Councillor Mrs Elaine Toghill.

▼ An impressive shot of Atlantic 75 B-712 Betty Battle, which served Hayling Island for the best part of fourteen years. (Nicholas Leach)

Two new lifeboats

▶ The 16ft 3in D class inflatable D-642 Amanda James and Ben on exercise, April 2007. Placed on station at Hayling Island in May 2005, she is an IB1 type boat powered by a 50hp outboard engine mounted on the transom. (Nicholas Leach)

I n May 2005 a new D class inshore lifeboat was sent to the station, and this was the start of the major upgrading of the station, which culminated four years later with a new Atlantic 85 and a new lifeboat station. The new D class cost £25,000 and was funded by Mrs Betty Battle, who had already paid for the station's Atlantic 75. The new boat was of the new IB1 type, and had a more powerful outboard engine than the older D class which gave a top speed of twenty-five knots.

The new boat was dedicated at a ceremony on 22 May 2005 when the boat was named after the donor's three grandchildren. At the start of the ceremony, Peter Glasby, Chairman of the station's Management Group, opened proceedings, and Mrs Battle's son, Jonathan, handed the boat over to the RNLI. Lifeboat Operations Manager Nigel Roper accepted the boat on behalf of the station, and then a service of dedication was conducted by the Rev Mary Thomas, the station's chaplain. At the end of the service, Amanda, James and Ben Battle jointly named the new ILB, which was launched for a short demonstration run.

▼ Naming ceremony of the D class inflatable D-642 Amanda James and Ben on 22 May 2005. (By courtesy of Ann Davies)

One of the first services in which the new ILB was involved took place on 3 July 2005. A crew member saw tyre marks leading towards the sea, and, after further investigations, it was thought a car may have been driven into the sea in the early hours. A nearby fishing boat was contacted and, with the echo sounder, the skipper confirmed something was on the sea bed. The position was marked, police divers were called and D-642 Amanda James and Ben was launched at 2.45pm. The diver went down at 3pm and found a car on the sea bed. The County tractor was brought to the scene and, using its winch, pulled the car from the sea. The vehicle, which was empty, was removed by a tow truck, and the ILB returned to station at 3.50pm.

On 23 July 2005, at about 1.30pm, B-712 Betty Battle was on a training exercise in the vicinity of the Ship Inn at Langstone, which was hosting the annual charity raft race. As the lifeboat crew was passing the bridge, they noticed someone pointing to a twelve-year-old boy in the water trapped by the rip tide against one of the bridge's piers. The boy had been fishing from the southern slip with a net and had slipped into the water where the current swept him onto the pier under the bridge and out of sight. The lifeboat crew immediately went to him, put the lifeboat alongside the pier and, with some difficulty because of the strong tidal stream, grabbed the boy and pulled him onto the lifeboat. He was treated by the lifeboat crew for shock and returned to the shore and into the care of a St John's Ambulance team. Unfortunately as it was high water the lifeboat sustained slight damage to her aerial and emergency light while manoeuvring under the bridge.

On 28 January 2006 both lifeboats were launched to a 26ft yacht, which was aground on the edge of West Pole Sands near the entrance to Chichester

▼ Atlantic 75 B-712 Betty Battle and D class inflatable D-642 Amanda James and Ben on exercise together. (Nicholas Leach)

▶ On exercise off Hayling Island, Atlantic 75 B-712 Betty Battle meets the Jubilee Sailing Trusts's 54m sail training ship Tenacious. (Nicholas Leach)

Harbour. The tide was falling and it was very cold, and the yacht's two crew were taken off by the D class. They were transferred to B-712 Betty Battle, which took them back to the lifeboat station and then returned to stand by the stranded yacht. Just after 3.30pm two lifeboat crew entered the water and boarded the yacht, which was floated off and towed to Chichester Harbour. The D class was relaunched at 4.05pm to take the yacht's crew to the Atlantic, which towed the yacht to Itchenor with two lifeboat crew on the yacht and the two men from the yacht on the lifeboat. The D class returned to station at 4.10pm and the Atlantic at 5.20pm.

Yachts and sailing dinghies are frequently in need of assistance, and on 27 May 2006 both Hayling lifeboats were launched when several sailing dinghies got into difficulty in Hayling Bay after being caught by an unexpected squall. Both lifeboats assisted several capsized dinghies and took a number of the sailors back to the lifeboat station, where some were treated for minor injuries. Some lifeboat crew also went into the water to help right the dinghies. The D class had to make a rapid return to the station with one sailor who was suffering from severe hypothermia. The lifeboat was beached, a manoeuvre only performed in emergency situations, so that the casualty could be carried by stretcher by the shore crew back to the boathouse, where he was treated by a paramedic until an ambulance arrived. Both lifeboats, a Coastguard helicopter and other boats in the area completed a thorough search until all the sailing dinghies and sailors were accounted for. The D class returned to station at 3pm and the Atlantic, after towing a dinghy with a broken mast back into the harbour, was recovered at 4.30pm.

On 29 August 2007 B-712 Betty Battle ended up helping three yachts after Solent Coastguard requested she go to the aid of a 42ft French yacht with engine failure thought to be anchored off West Wittering Beach, whose skipper was unfamiliar with the area. En route, the lifeboat crew found another yacht in difficulty on West Pole sands. It was aground but in no imminent danger, so the lifeboat crew laid an anchor for it to await the rising tide and then went to the French yacht. Once they reached it, a line was rigged and the vessel was towed to Chichester Harbour. On returning to the lifeboat station, the lifeboat crew spotted another yacht aground and towed it to deeper water. The lifeboat then returned to station at 6.50pm.

Both lifeboats are often taken out on training exercises, and occasionally the boats are tasked on service when already at sea. On 26 September 2007, shortly after launching on exercise, B-712 Betty Battle was asked to investigate a report from a ferry that a submerged object showing a white light had been seen about 400 metres south of the Saddle Buoy at the entrance to Portsmouth Harbour. On reaching the scene, the lifeboat searched an area towards Southsea but found nothing. At 8.47pm the lifeboat was released and went back to station, but ten minutes later the Coastguard reported that a life jacket with a light attached had been found off St Helen's Fort.

During 2005 plans were made for the stationing of a new Atlantic 85 at Hayling. The boat would replace B-712 Betty Battle, but due to her size a larger boathouse was needed. Tractors had been supplied to launch both lifeboats since the previous station had been built, replacing the winches used since the first ILBs came to the station. Therefore, any new boathouse would also

◀ The temporary station in the car park close to the lifeboat house accommodated the lifeboats, launching tractors, and equipment while the boathouse was being rebuilt. (Nicholas Leach)

▼ Two photos showing various stages of the rebuilding of the ILB house during 2007. (Nigel Roper)

▶ Atlantic 75 B-712
Betty Battle is launched
on exercise by County
MB 764 tractor TW43,
which served the station
from 1998 to 2008.
(Nicholas Leach)

have to accommodate the vehicles so they could be permanently coupled to the lifeboat launching trolleys to expedite launching and improve safety procedures. Shoehorning the tractors and boats into a boathouse which was too small required much skill, and it was far from satisfactory. Various proposals were considered, but the most suitable one was to extensively rebuild the existing boathouse. Work began on the rebuilding in late 2006 and progressed well during the summer. Throughout the building work, the lifeboats remained operational. They were kept in containers in the adjacent car park, which also provided rudimentary facilities for the crews.

In November 2007 the new boathouse was completed and over the weekend of 1-2 December 2007 the lifeboats and equipment were moved into the new facility. The building consisted of a 19m by 11m boat hall, with an upper storey for the operations room and office. The original boathouse, which was incorporated into the new building, was rearranged to provide a dedicated training and education facility, a changing room and a museum for visitors. The new boat hall was large enough for both lifeboats and their respective launching vehicles to be coupled together in line, something that had not been possible in the previous house, and reduced launch times.

On 25 June 2008 the lifeboat launched to a capsized catamaran dinghy in Chichester Harbour. The crew of a passing yacht saw a man, who had fallen out of the dinghy when his trapeze line broke, clinging to a navigation post. The dinghy, with the other crewman still on board, had then capsized but its occupant had managed to reach the beach. The passing yacht was unable to get close due to the shallow water, but the lifeboat soon reached the man clinging to the post, who was by now exhausted, and took him aboard the lifeboat. A lifeboat crew member then helped the helm of the catamaran to sail his boat back to Thorney Island, escorted by the lifeboat with the other dinghy sailor on board. B-712 Betty Battle returned to station at 6.50pm.

Every year an Open Day is held at the station so that visitors can look round the facilities and see the lifeboats in action, but during the 2008 Open Day, held on 13 July 2008, the B-712 Betty Battle was tasked to three separate incidents rather than undertaking routine demonstrations for the crowds. The first incident was at 11am, when the lifeboat crew carried out a medical evacuation of a young boy from a yacht at anchor off East Head in Chichester Harbour. The boy had cut his foot whilst walking on the beach and had a bad wound. At 12.45pm the Atlantic 75 went to assist a fishing boat that had broken down in Hayling Bay, and towed the boat to safety. At 2.15pm the lifeboat launched to a sports boat off Bracklesham Bay that had lost her propeller, and towed that boat into the harbour.

The lifeboat was involved in an unusual incident on 6 August 2008 when Solent Coastguard requested the lifeboat go to West Wittering beach where a large crowd had gathered on the beach, and some people were in the water, after reports that a pod of whales had stranded on the sand bank. It was soon realised that the whales were in fact shifting sand and waves, and the lifeboat was stood down and returned to station.

The most notable event of 2009 was the arrival, on 24 February, of the new Atlantic 85, B-829. B-712 Betty Battle was returned to the RNLI Depot at Poole, and subsequently sold out of service. After two days of intense crew training had been completed on the Atlantic 85, the new boat was placed on station. She was launched on service for the first time the day she arrived, being tasked by Solent Coastguard to stand by a yacht that had broken down off Selsey, which eventually made here own way into Chichester harbour. The new Atlantic 85 soon proved to have a remarkably enhanced sea-keeping capability over her predecessor.

▼ Atlantic 85 B-829 Derrick Battle is put through her paces during a training exercise on 25 February 2009, the day after she arrived on station. The Atlantic 85 is the latest development of the RNLI's B class, and is fitted with radar interlaced with GPS and VHF direction-finding equipment, is powered by two 115hp outboard engines giving a top speed of thirty-five knots. (Nicholas Leach)

Replacing B-712 and named Derrick Battle, B-829 was the third lifeboat to be donated by Betty Battle. The association between Betty Battle and the Hayling station started when Betty was given a sum of money by her husband Derrick on his retirement in 1995, 'to do with as she pleased'. Betty was a past chairman of the RNLI's Ashtead Branch and she wanted to assist the RNLI, who suggested she should fund a new Atlantic 75 for Hayling Island, costing £70,000. A friendship with the station developed, and when Derrick passed away in 1997 Betty started to save for a new D class ILB, which arrived in 2005 and was named for her grandchildren. Sadly, Betty died on 1 October 2006 after a long illness, but she arranged for the replacement of B-712 to be named after her husband. In recognition of her most generous and personal support for the station, and to ensure that her name should continue to be remembered, the County launching tractor has been named Betty.

▶ Atlantic 75 B-712 Betty Battle with her successor B-829 Derrick Battle on 25 February 2009. (Nicholas Leach)

▼ The three Battle-funded lifeboats together outside the lifeboat house: D-642 Amanda, James and Ben, B-712 Betty Battle and B-829 Derrick Battle. (Nicholas Leach)

◀ The impressive lifeboat station at Hayling Island completed in 2007 to house both Atlantic 85 and D class inshore lifeboats, as well as the respective launch vehicles. Above the boat hall is a large and well-equipped training room, while the north part of the building (on right) is part of the 1995 boathouse. The boathouse extension was funded from legacies of around £500,000 from the Lusty family and the remaining £300,000 provided by Gwendoline Prince and Mr and Mrs Hudson. (Andrew Filipinski)

The new Atlantic 85 was named on 25 April 2009, when the extended boathouse was also dedicated. Peter Glasby, Chairman of the station's management group, opened the proceedings and welcomed about 350 people to the celebrations. Derrick and Betty's son Jonathan, and one of their granddaughters, Amanda Chitty, handed over the lifeboat to Rear Admiral Stacey, CBE, who was representing the RNLI. Accepting it on their behalf, he then in turn handed it to Nigel Roper, Lifeboat Operations Manager.

Rev Mary Thomas, station chaplain, conducted the service of dedication and at the end of the ceremony, James Chitty, the donor's eldest grandson, named the new lifeboat Derrick Battle after his grandfather. During the ceremony, Rear Admiral Stacey also accepted the new boathouse, which had been funded by three bequests from the estates of Ray and Audrey Lusty, Bruce and Margaret Hudson and Gwendoline Prince. Present at the ceremony were representatives of the legators, a nephew of Mrs Prince, John Grumbridge (who was also a member of the crew) and Pippa Stevens, the daughter of Mr and Mrs Hudson, who unveiled a commemorative plaque. The boathouse was formally handed to Nigel Roper by the Admiral. Subsequently, the second tractor was named Gwendoline.

The year that the Atlantic 85 arrived proved to be one of the busiest in the history of the station, with the lifeboats undertaking a total of 121 services. One of the most testing incidents came on 25 July 2009. As the lifeboats were about to be recovered after an exercise, a Mayday was received from a yacht in Hayling Bay stating that the skipper had fallen overboard. His wife had thrown a line to him, but she could not get him back aboard and was unsure of their position. As well as the lifeboats, Hayling Rescue, a private safety boat operated by an ex-lifeboat crewman, Frank Dunster, responded to the call, and a lifeboat crew member was transferred on to Hayling Rescue to assist its skipper, who was on his own.

▶ Atlantic 85 B-829 Derrick Battle being launched on exercise, March 2010. The Atlantic 85 is manned by a crew of four, one more than the previous rigid-inflatable inshore lifeboats to serve the station. (Nicholas Leach)

Hayling Rescue was first on scene, with the lifeboat crew member going into the water to assist the casualty. Using a knife from Hayling Rescue, the casualty's wife cut the line and her husband was assisted on to Hayling Rescue. The casualty was then transferred to the Atlantic 85, taken back to the lifeboat station and later taken to hospital by ambulance as he was hypothermic, having been in the water for forty-five minutes. Hayling Rescue, with help from the lifeboat crew, then towed the yacht into Sparkes Marina and the casualty's wife was taken by lifeboat to the lifeboat station.

The lifeboats launched again later that day, at 5.21pm, after the Coastguard requested assistance with the transfer of a man to an ambulance after the man had fallen off a coastal footpath and broken his leg. The ambulance was unable to get near the casualty so he was taken in the D class inflatable D-642 and, with the assistance of the lifeboat crew on B-829 Derrick Battle, transferred to a waiting ambulance at Northney Marina. The lifeboats returned to station at 6.26pm.

On 22 August 2009 both lifeboats were involved in a long service. B-829 Derrick Battle launched to a vessel aground on the West Pole Sands. Once on scene, the Atlantic's crew requested the D class inflatable because the

▼ James Chitty pours champagne over the bow of B-829 Derrick Battle during the naming ceremony of the Atlantic 85, 25 April 2009. (Andrew Filipinski)

casualty was in such shallow water. The D class launched at 9.44pm and its crew helped get the vessel off. The casualty was then escorted by both lifeboats to harbour. As she made her own way up harbour, it became clear that the skipper had no local knowledge and the senior helmsman on the Atlantic decided to escort the vessel to Emsworth, where she was placed on moorings.

On 5 October 2009 both lifeboats were launched just after 7pm to go to the aid of a 62-year-old man after he fell from his catamaran

◄ The children and grandchildren of Derrick and Betty Battle at the naming ceremony of the new Atlantic 85. They are, from left to right, Jonathan Battle, Mia Battle, James Chitty, Amanda Chitty and Sailly Chitty, with Ben Battle in front. (Andrew Filipinski)

◄ The senior helmsmen at the naming of B-829, 25 April 2009; left to right, Ian Fiddaman, Paul Lewis and Andrew Ferguson. (Andrew Filipinski)

when his rope ladder broke. He fell into shallow water and got stuck in the mud in Chichester Harbour. With the tide rising around him he was unable to get back into his boat, so he used his mobile phone to call the Coastguard. Within five minutes both lifeboats were on scene. Lifeboat crew members heard his cries for help and found him in the shallow, muddy water clinging to his boat. The casualty had been in the water for around thirty minutes and was suffering from hypothermia, so he was quickly taken back to the lifeboat station by the Atlantic 85 where a paramedic and shore crew members attended him until an ambulance arrived. The Atlantic 85 returned to the area to tow the catamaran to Sparkes Marina, where it was made safe. Andy Ferguson, Hayling Island Senior Helmsman said: 'The gentleman from Worthing was incredibly lucky that his mobile phone, which was not in

▶ Lifeboat crew on board B-829 Derrick Battle during the annual raft race organised by The Ship public house at Langstone. The event sees a dozen or so home-made craft compete to raise money for charity, and the RNLI usually benefits by sums of around £3,000. On duty here are Jasper Graham-Jones, Andrew Altendorff, Craig Elsdon (Helmsman), Matthew Farr, Steven Hulatt, Jamie Stickler, Ian Fiddaman (Senior Helmsman). (Nicholas Leach)

a waterproof case, remained dry and workable when he fell into the water. There was no one around who would have heard his cries and with the tide rising he would have been in severe difficulty.'

The following day B-829 Derrick Battle was in action again. She launched on 6 October 2009 to a yacht which had suffered an engine fire and lost all power, while the jib was also jammed. Once on scene, the casualty was taken in tow by the Chichester Harbour Master's patrol vessel and the lifeboat crew were stood down. The lifeboat retuned to station at 12.35pm.

When both lifeboats were called out on Sunday 18 October 2009, it was the 100th incident of the year, something of a milestone. The boats were called to a family in a dinghy which had run aground in shallow water with a falling tide near the entrance to Chichester Harbour. D-642 Amanda, James and Ben launched at 3.30pm and took the mother and four-year-old child, who were very cold, on board the lifeboat and towed the dinghy into deeper water. B-829 Derrick Battle was also launched to assist and took over the tow, bringing the boat to Itchenor. Meanwhile the D class inflatable was tasked to the 101st incident, assisting a 22ft yacht that was also aground near the entrance to Chichester Harbour.

The rescue of the family on the speedboat was one of nineteen incidents that day which required both Hayling Island lifeboats, and the 121 call-outs during 2009 was a record for the station. The commitment and dedication of the volunteer lifeboat crew has been the hallmark of the station's success, and the current crews are latest in a long line of Hayling Islanders willing to give up their own time and risk their own safety to help save lives at sea. During the years of its operation, up until 31 December 2009, the Hayling Island lifeboats have saved a total of 489 lives.

Lifeboat summary

On station	Official Number	Name Donor	Dimensions Type
Pulling lifeboats			
9.1865 – 4.1888		**Olive Leaf** Messrs Leaf & Sons, London.	32ft x 7ft 5in Self-righter
4.1888 – 5.1914	146	**Charlie and Adrian** Gift of L. T. Cave, Ditcham Park.	34ft x 7ft 6in Self-righter
5.1914 – 9.1924	640	**Proctor** Gift of William John Proctor, Newcastle.	35ft x 8ft 10in Rubie self-righter
Atlantic inshore lifeboats			
3.1975 – 10.1980	B-511	**Co-Operative No.1** Co-operative Women's Guild.	22ft 9in x 7ft 6in Atlantic 21
10.1980 – 10.1994	B-548	**Aldershot** Aldershot Branch, and legacy of Doris Marjorie Chartres.	22ft 9in x 7ft 6in Atlantic 21
6.10.1994 – 1.1995	B-541	**Elizabeth Bestwick** Bequest of Miss Edith A. Bestwick.	22ft 9in x 7ft 6in Atlantic 21
11.1.1995 – 6.1995	B-526	**(Un-named)** Lady D. E. G. Hunt.	22ft 9in x 7ft 6in Atlantic 21
21.6.1995 – 2.2009	B-712	**Betty Battle** Gift of Mr and Mrs Derrick Battle, Ashtead, Surrey.	24ft x 8ft 8in Atlantic 75
26.2.2009 –	B-829	**Derrick Battle** Gift of Mrs Betty Battle, Ashtead.	8.3m x 2.8m Atlantic 85
D class inflatable inshore lifeboats			
29.3.1995 – 3.1996	D-398	**Victory Wheelers** Victory Wheelers Custom Car Club.	16ft 3in x 6ft 7in Avon EA16
12.3.1996 – 5.2005	D-496	**Leonard Stedman** Farnham Branch RNLI.	16ft 3in x 6ft 7in Avon EA16
24.5.2005 –	D-642	**Amanda James and Ben** Gift of Mrs Betty Battle, Ashtead.	16ft 3in x 6ft 7in IB1

▶ Hayling Island's lifeboats, from left to right, D-642 Amanda James and Ben, B-712 Betty Battle and B-829 Derrick Battle passing the lifeboat house at Sandy Point. (Nicholas Leach)

Services 1865–1924

Year	Date	Casualty	Outcome

Olive Leaf lifeboat (1865-1888)

Year	Date	Casualty	Outcome
1865	Oct 29	Barque Atlas, of North Shields	Saved 13 and assisted to save vessel
		Norwegian barque Sirius, of Christiania	Saved (from Atlas) 1
1866	Feb 11	Brig Johanna Elisabeth, of Hamburg	No effective service
1867	Feb 8	Brigantine Maria Crowell, of Halifax, Nova Scotia	No effective service
1869	Feb 1	Barque Lady Westmorland, of Newcastle	Assisted to save barque and 18
1870	Oct 13	Brig Lisbon, of Glasgow	Took out pilot and assisted to save brig
1881	Nov 20	Barque Caducens, of North Shields	Launched, but unable to assist
1882	July 23	Unknown schooner	Services not required
1883	Feb 2	Brig Tearful, of Portsmouth	Could not locate vessel
1888	Mar 11	Barque Alivia, of Norway	No effective service

Charlie and Adrian Lifeboat (1888-1914)

Year	Date	Casualty	Outcome
1888	July 20	Barque Margit, of Norway	No effective service
1889	Feb 18	Naval torpedo boat	No effective service
1894	Feb 26	Unknown vessel	No effective service
1896	Jan 14	Brigantine Marie Louise, of Quebec	Stood by
1897	Apr 2	Schooner General Havelock, of Portsmouth	No effective service
1900	Nov 12	Ketch Georgina, of Poole	No effective service
1903	Mar 2	Ketch Seraphus, of Plymouth	No effective service
	Sep 11	Cutter yacht Dodo	No effective service
1905	Aug 20	Motor yacht Cruban, of Glasgow	No effective service
1906	Feb 8	Barge Mabel, of Portsmouth	Saved 2
1908	Aug 31	Unknown vessel	No effective service
	Sep 1	Schooner Ageuoria, of Chester	No effective service
1909	Dec 10	Ketch Birthday, of London	No effective service
1910	Oct 3	Barge Sylvia	No effective service
	Dec 14	Italian brigantine Fratelli Lama	Services not required
	Dec 16	Schooner Blanche, of Dunkirk	Saved 7
1912	Nov 25	Smack Burt, of Bosham	No effective service
1913	Mar 19	Schooner Rescue, of London	No effective service

Proctor Lifeboat (1914-1924)

Year	Date	Casualty	Outcome
1916	Dec 15	Steam tug Morino	Crew assembled
1920	Jan 10	Schooner Monte Grande, of Havre	Saved 15
	June 20	Royal Fleet Auxiliary tanker Plumleaf, of London	Stood by
1922	Sep 26	Yacht Madge	Nothing found after search
1923	Aug 26	Yacht Quick Step, of Hayling Island	No effective service

Total lives saved by pulling and sailing lifeboats = 38

ILB service summary

Year	First launch	ILB	Launches	Launches/lives saved
1975	16 Mar	B-511	43	**43 / 35**
1976	15 May	B-511	43	**43 / 29**
1977	5 Feb	B-511	38	**38 / 5**
1978	2 Jan	B-511	22	**22 / 11**
1979	3 Mar	B-511	22	**25 / 19**
	3 Nov	B-525	3	
1980	9 Feb	B-525	21	**30 / 14**
	5 Oct	B-511	4	
	15 Nov	B-548	5	
1981	7 Mar	B-548	43	**43 / 15**
1982	2 Jan	B-548	58	**58 / 17**
1983	15 Jan	B-548	67	**67 / 36**
1984	19 Feb	B-548	42	**42 / 9**
1985	1 Jan	B-541	41	**41 / 23**
1986	20 Apr	B-548	36	**36 / 7**
1987	4 Jan	B-548	56	**58 / 15**
	14 Sep	B-515	2	
1988	17 Jan	B-548	46	**48 / 16**
	9 Oct	B-526	2	
1989	21 Jan	B-548	56	**57 / 25**
	4 Jun	B-526	1	
1990	19 Jan	B-548	5	**52 / 7**
	19 Feb	B-532	14	
	14 Jul	B-538	15	
	8 Aug	B-548	18	
1991	7 Jan	B-548	54	**54 / 15**
1992	16 Feb	B-548	59	**60 / 33**
	12 Nov	B-527	1	
1993	21 Jan	B-548	73	**73 / 31**
1994	3 Jan	B-548	17	**73 / 10**
	2 May	B-541	22	
	17 Jul	B-555	7	
	31 Jul	B-541	27	
1995	15 Jan	B-700	3	**101 / 38**
	11 Feb	B-526	17	
	1 Apr	D-398	44	
	9 Jul	B-712	37	
1996	22 Jan	B-712	81	**122 / 24**
	22 Mar	D-496	41	
1997	19 Jan	B-712	71	**97 / 29**
	19 Jan	D-496	26	
1998	8 Feb	B-712	67	**94 / 16**
	8 Feb	D-496	27	
1999	6 Feb	B-712	19	**66 / 14**
	7 Mar	D-496	2	
	1 May	D-488	5	
	5 Jun	B-736	28	
	10 Jul	D-496	12	
2000	2 Jan	B-736	2	**68 / 2**
	9 Apr	B-712	54	
	14 May	D-496	10	
	12 Nov	D-483	2	
2001	21 Jan	B-712	58	**82 / 13**
	3 Feb	D-496	15	
	31 Jul	D-500	8	
	27 Oct	D-496	1	
2002	5 Jan	B-712	26	**53 / 7**
	16 Feb	D-496	14	
	14 Jul	B-713	5	
	10 Aug	B-712	8	
2003	23 Jan	D-496	8	**92 / 0**
	23 Jan	D-465	8	
	12 Feb	B-712	54	
	12 Apr	B-757	9	
	12 Jul	D-423	13	
2004	9 Jan	D-496	19	**92 / 3**
	9 Jan	B-712	53	
	7 Feb	B-792	14	
	19 Sep	D-465	6	
2005	9 Jan	B-712	36	**61 / 0**
	14 Feb	D-496	3	
	25 Mar	B-754	4	
	27 May	D-642	18	
2006	1 Jan	B-712	42	**86 / 2**
	28 Jan	D-642	28	
	12 Jul	B-734	14	
	20 Nov	D-655	2	
2007	6 Jan	B-712	42	**65 / 0**
	31 Jan	D-655	1	
	12 May	D-642	22	
2008	6 Jan	B-712	47	**77 / 1**
	19 Jan	D-642	30	
2009	4 Jan	B-712	4	**121 / 11**
	17 Jan	D-642	57	
	24 Feb	B-829	60	

The following ILBs served on relief duty at various times:
B-525 Spix's Macaw • B-555 Long Life I • B-700 Susan Peacock • B-713 OEM Stone • B-734 Amy Constance • B-736 Toshiba Wave Warrior • D-465 Palmer Bayer • D-483 C John Morris DFM • D-488 Mabel • D-500 • D-655 Guardian Angel

Personnel

Honorary Secretaries

Rev Charles Hardy	1865 – 1880
William Payne	1880 – 1887
Henry Trigg	1887 – 1901
Frederick Trigg	1901 – 1907
Walter Howell	1907 – 1916
Captain R. W. Neate	1916 – 1919
Henry West	1919 – 1924
Station closed 1924 – 1975	
Frank Martin	1975 – 1978
Roy Smith	1978 – 1988
Brian Read	1988 – 1996
Nigel Roper	1996 –

Deputy Launching Authorities

Sir David Mackworth, Roy Smith, Basil Rizzi, Lieut Cmdr Charles Errington, Brian Read, Paddy Lamperd, Nigel Roper, Peter Glasby, Ron Caldicott, Cmdr Conrad Davies, Jonathan Bradbury, Gil Carter, Keith Holmes, Nick Willis and Graham Raines

Coxswains

William Goldring }	1865 – 1880
James Spraggs }	
Stephen Goldring*	1880 – 1892
George Thomas Miller	1892 – 1919
Charles Henry Cole	1919 – 1924
*Superintendent Coxswain	

Senior Helmsmen

Paddy Lamperd	1975 – 1988
Tony Gardiner	1975 – 1978
Mike Mountifield	1975 – 1980
Frank Dunster	1975 – 1995
Mike Murray	1977 – 1983
Ross Hornsby	1977 – 1981
Rod James	1983 – 1997
Simon Wilson	1989 – 1992
Graham Raines	1992 – 2004
Robert Briggs	1995 – 2006
Damien Taylor	1997 – 2001
Ian Harris	2001 – 2007
Paul Lewis	2004 –
Ian Fiddaman	2004 –
John Robinson	2006 – 2007
Andrew Ferguson	2007 –

▼ Lifeboat Operations Manager Nigel Roper with the Atlantic 85 Derrick Battle. Nigel joined the station as a shore helper in 1977, became a Deputy Launchng Authority in 1990 as well as Press Officer, and in 1996 was appointed as Honorary Secretary, a title subsequently changed to Lifeboat Operations Manager. During his long service to the RNLI, he has been closely involved with the evolution of the station from the early days to the current impressive set-up. (Nicholas Leach)

Because of the large number of services performed by the Hayling lifeboats, and because crews also have to train and exercise, soon after the station reopened in the 1970s sufficient crew were recruited so that three separate watches could be operated, with each watch performing duty for one week. Thus the senior helmsmen's period of service overlaps in the above listing.